BOKO HARAM: THE GROWING THREAT TO SCHOOLGIRLS, NIGERIA, AND BEYOND

HEARING

BEFORE THE

COMMITTEE ON FOREIGN AFFAIRS
HOUSE OF REPRESENTATIVES

ONE HUNDRED THIRTEENTH CONGRESS

SECOND SESSION

MAY 21, 2014

Serial No. 113–172

Printed for the use of the Committee on Foreign Affairs

Available via the World Wide Web: http://www.foreignaffairs.house.gov/ or
http://www.gpo.gov/fdsys/

U.S. GOVERNMENT PRINTING OFFICE

88–018PDF   WASHINGTON : 2014

For sale by the Superintendent of Documents, U.S. Government Printing Office
Internet: bookstore.gpo.gov   Phone: toll free (866) 512–1800; DC area (202) 512–1800
Fax: (202) 512–2104   Mail: Stop IDCC, Washington, DC 20402–0001

COMMITTEE ON FOREIGN AFFAIRS

EDWARD R. ROYCE, California, *Chairman*

CHRISTOPHER H. SMITH, New Jersey
ILEANA ROS-LEHTINEN, Florida
DANA ROHRABACHER, California
STEVE CHABOT, Ohio
JOE WILSON, South Carolina
MICHAEL T. McCAUL, Texas
TED POE, Texas
MATT SALMON, Arizona
TOM MARINO, Pennsylvania
JEFF DUNCAN, South Carolina
ADAM KINZINGER, Illinois
MO BROOKS, Alabama
TOM COTTON, Arkansas
PAUL COOK, California
GEORGE HOLDING, North Carolina
RANDY K. WEBER SR., Texas
SCOTT PERRY, Pennsylvania
STEVE STOCKMAN, Texas
RON DeSANTIS, Florida
DOUG COLLINS, Georgia
MARK MEADOWS, North Carolina
TED S. YOHO, Florida

ELIOT L. ENGEL, New York
ENI F.H. FALEOMAVAEGA, American
  Samoa
BRAD SHERMAN, California
GREGORY W. MEEKS, New York
ALBIO SIRES, New Jersey
GERALD E. CONNOLLY, Virginia
THEODORE E. DEUTCH, Florida
BRIAN HIGGINS, New York
KAREN BASS, California
WILLIAM KEATING, Massachusetts
DAVID CICILLINE, Rhode Island
ALAN GRAYSON, Florida
JUAN VARGAS, California
BRADLEY S. SCHNEIDER, Illinois
JOSEPH P. KENNEDY III, Massachusetts
AMI BERA, California
ALAN S. LOWENTHAL, California
GRACE MENG, New York
LOIS FRANKEL, Florida
TULSI GABBARD, Hawaii
JOAQUIN CASTRO, Texas

AMY PORTER, *Chief of Staff*   THOMAS SHEEHY, *Staff Director*

JASON STEINBAUM, *Democratic Staff Director*

(II)

CONTENTS

BOKO HARAM: THE GROWING THREAT TO SCHOOLGIRLS, NIGERIA, AND BEYOND

WEDNESDAY, MAY 21, 2014

HOUSE OF REPRESENTATIVES,
COMMITTEE ON FOREIGN AFFAIRS,
Washington, DC.

The committee met, pursuant to notice, at 9:53 a.m., in room 2172, Rayburn House Office Building, Hon. Ed Royce (chairman of the committee) presiding.

Chairman ROYCE. This hearing will come to order.

Today, as we meet here, we have nearly 300 young girls from Chibok, in Northern Nigeria, that remain Boko Haram kidnap victims.

It has been 5 weeks since they were abducted. Every passing minute makes their successful rescue less likely. And we meet today to ensure that the United States is doing everything it can to assist in their rescue. Just yesterday, the House passed a resolution pressing for more aggressive action.

Many around the world are just now hearing of Boko Haram. Sadly, though, for communities in Northern Nigeria, they know the death and destruction that this group brings only too well, and they have known it for a number of years.

They have known it for a number of years because, as Boko Haram has spread, they have continued to burn schools. As of today, over 500 schools have been destroyed. Over 100 teachers have been killed.

This morning committee members had the chance to meet with Deborah Peter. Deborah, a young woman of just 15 years of age, is from Chibok, Nigeria, the same town where the recent abductions took place. Ms. Peter is seated in the front row. She is one of only three Boko Haram survivors in the United States. She courageously shared her traumatic experience at the hands of Boko Haram with us this morning. Her father and her brother—her father was a pastor—were executed in front of her eyes for not renouncing their Christian faith. His church was burned to the ground. We thank Deborah for being with us today. We thank her and her friends for traveling from rural Virginia to share her traumatic story in the hopes that the world will act.

We are faced with two challenges in Northern Nigeria; in the near term, seeing these girls rescued, and in the long term, rendering Boko Haram unable to threaten the region. This is a group that has killed thousands, thousands, of Nigerians to date. And their loose title of the translation ''Boko Haram'' is ''Western education is a sin.'' Their mission is to carry out a war against those who educate or empower women. And the greatest sin to them is not treating women as chattel, which they do, or enslaving women, which they purport to justify, or selling women. No. The greatest sin to them is to be involved in educating or teaching young women how to read and write.

And over time this group, Boko Haram, has developed a vast arsenal of weapons. They are an al-Qaeda affiliate. They have sworn their allegiance to al-Qaeda. They have received training from al-Qaeda groups. They have built up their resources with that support. And this means greater terror for the people in Northern Nigeria and greater challenges for Nigerian security forces.

Unfortunately, these forces suffer unprofessional elements with poor morale. I have been in Nigeria several times. It is a struggle for the Nigerian military to cope with this threat, which has led some to say that we should not get involved. But it tells me otherwise. It tells me that U.S. involvement is critical. U.S. forces are well positioned to advise and assist. We can advise and assist Nigerian forces in the search and the rescue of these girls. In this role, U.S. forces expertly trained to deal with hostage situations, jungle environments, and in tracking could help Nigerians with intelligence, planning, and logistics. If some U.S. laws would hinder such assistance, the administration should use its waiver authority under these extraordinary circumstances.

Why do we care? We care about Deborah, her friends and family. We care about a girl's right to an education. We care about human rights and religious liberty and the future of Africa's largest country, largest in population, largest economy.

We have direct security interests. Commanders at the Pentagon have stated that Boko Haram is, in their words, a ''threat to Western interests'' and one of the highest counterterrorism priorities in Africa.

Pressure from this committee was critical in getting the State Department to designate Boko Haram as a Foreign Terrorist Organization. Indeed, the administration made that announcement in this room under pressure from us on this committee.

As many have noted, it shouldn't have taken so long. We want to hear from the State Department and the Pentagon witnesses on the strategy we now have in place.

Boko Haram, with heavy weapons and grenade attacks, is waging a brutal war against schoolgirls carrying backpacks, books, and pencils. We can't sit on the sidelines.

And I will now turn to the ranking member for his opening comments, Mr. Eliot Engel of New York.

Mr. ENGEL. Thank you, Mr. Chairman. And thank you for holding this very timely hearing on Boko Haram.

I would like to thank our witnesses, Dr. Sewall and Ms. Dory, for being here today.

And, of course, I would like to welcome Ms. Deborah Peter, a brave young survivor of a Boko Haram attack in 2011. She met with members of this committee earlier this morning to describe her harrowing experience.

Deborah, we are all grateful for your courage and your commitment to seeing that these horrible abuses are stopped so that no other family goes through what your family has gone through. Thank you for your courage. We are all very, very proud of you.

And I must also say, since I had the opportunity to meet with her privately, how proud any parent would be of having a daughter like Deborah.

So thank you, Deborah.

Mr. Chairman, Boko Haram is an Islamic extremist group, increasingly active since 2010. It operates mainly in Northern Nigeria.

As we all know, one of Boko Haram's most recent atrocities took place on April 14 of this year. That day nearly 300 schoolgirls were doing what young women and girls all over the world do every day, studying for tests, playing with friends, building a future for themselves.

That day Boko Haram, which roughly translates to ''Western education is forbidden,'' abducted these girls; tore them away from their families and their communities.

Today, more than a month later, we still don't know where they are. Our thoughts are obviously with their families, and we pray that they are safely reunited as soon as possible.

The United States and other international partners have offered assistance to bring the schoolgirls home, and we all hope those efforts will prove successful.

I agree with Chairman Royce that we must do everything in our power to bring those girls home and the United States can be very helpful in assisting this process.

But even as we work to address the crisis, we need to focus on the larger challenge: Stopping Boko Haram's reign of terror in Nigeria and beyond.

Just yesterday Boko Haram set off two bombs in the city of Jos, killing over 100 people—100 innocent people. Two weeks ago the group attacked a market in the town of Gamboru, killing more than 300 people.

Back in 2011, in one of their most high-profile attacks, the terrorist group bombed the United Nations' headquarters in Abuja, killing at least 21 people and injuring more than 120. You really have to be bold to attack a United Nations headquarters.

So, all told, Boko Haram has murdered more than 5,000 people over the last 4 years. Their victims are both Christians and Muslims, men, women, and children, and, of course, teachers.

Before this brazen kidnapping, Boko Haram was virtually unknown around the world. As more of their violent history has come to light, the international community has reacted with shock, horror and disbelief. But the sad reality is that Boko Haram is not new and neither are their tactics.

I think our witnesses can shed more light on the situation for us and for everyone following the plight of these young girls.

How did Boko Haram emerge and grow into an extremist threat? What has allowed them to thrive as on organization? And what challenges does the U.S. face in working with Nigeria to disrupt and dismantle the group?

Let me just say, contrary to some of the reporting I have seen, I know the difficulty in weakening Boko Haram has not been due to a lack of effort or an unwillingness to help.

In fact, one of our major challenges is working with the Nigerian military itself. Its approach in Northern Nigeria has often alienated the very population that could be providing valuable information about Boko Haram's activities.

But instead of forming these relationships, unfortunately, the military has too often built a record of indiscriminate destruction themselves, theft of personal property, arbitrary arrests, indefinite detention, torture, and extrajudicial killing of civilians, much of this with impunity.

In addition, despite a recent intelligence-sharing agreement, there are legitimate concerns that intelligence shared with the military to assist them in their operations might be leaked. And to make matters worse, this corruption is rampant throughout the force. Nigerian security forces are the best funded on the African continent. Yet, many of the funds are siphoned off by corruption and troops often aren't paid a living wage, generating increased frustration in the ranks and fueling low-level corruption.

So how exactly can the U.S. engage with a military force that sometimes lacks professionalism and often seems to fail with respect to human rights? And how do we convince Nigerian leaders that they aren't doing enough and, in fact, may be making the problem worse?

Lastly, while we are very focused on recovering these girls and stopping Boko Haram, we need to look at the broader context.

Years of economic stagnation and neglect have afflicted Northern Nigeria and created the sort of environment where terrorist groups thrive.

In places where there is no support or opportunity, extremists find it easier to prey on vulnerable populations, preaching false ideologies of violence and hatred.

To push back against this tide, I believe Nigeria's Government must address these issues of corruption by improving the professionalism of its security forces, and providing additional resources for education, infrastructure, and economic activity. In short, Nigeria must take a more holistic approach to counterterrorism.

I look forward to hearing from our witnesses about how the U.S. can more effectively engage with the Nigerians when addressing the scourge of Boko Haram today.

I regard Nigeria as our partner in this, and the United States needs to be helpful to them. We need to build an environment that forces development and prosperity in Northern Nigeria for tomorrow.

So thank you, Mr. Chairman, for holding this hearing.

And thanks to the witnesses and Deborah for appearing here today.

I yield back.

Chairman ROYCE. Thank you, Mr. Engel.

We go to Mr. Chris Smith, chair of the Africa subcommittee, for 1 minute.

Mr. SMITH. Thank you very much, Mr. Chairman. And, again, thank you very much for convening this extremely important hearing.

Obviously, words are inadequate to express our concern—and I say that collectively for all of us—for the welfare and whereabouts of the abducted girls, as well as the outrage toward Boko Haram for this absolutely horrific act of aggression and violence against these young women.

My good friend and colleague, Mr. Engel, just mentioned how Boko Haram was largely unknown around the world until this infamous incident, but not to Chairman Royce or Eliot Engel or Ranking Member Bass or me or any other member of this committee.

We have been raising the concerns of Boko Haram for years. Especially since 2011, when they seemed to transition into a more lethal stage with the bombing of the U.N. mission in Abuja, but, also, the very real problem of not being designated a Foreign Terrorist Organization.

I held two hearings on Boko Haram. Emmanuel Ogebe was at one of those hearings. As a matter of fact, I went with him. He joined us in Jos and in Abuja. We met with people who had been victims of fire bombings, and Christians as well as some Muslims, who were targeted for killings by these thugs.

He made it very clear then—he is now accompanying Deborah Peter—how this is only going to get worse unless all means are used to destroy this terrible threat.

And it took years to get the designation of the Foreign Terrorist Organization (FTO). I am looking forward to what the answer may be. It wasn't until we had another hearing that it was announced that, yes, it would be designated a FTO.

I don't know—I still can't understand what the delay was when—I asked Ambassador Johnnie Carson repeatedly at one of those hearings—and that is the one that Mr. Ogebe testified at—why? Why the delay?

I mean, we all need to be on the same page now and work as never before to assist the Government of Nigeria. But we lost some precious time, in all candor, by not designating Boko Hara as a Foreign Terrorist Organization earlier rather than later.

Yield back.

Chairman ROYCE. Thank you.

Congresswoman Karen Bass isn't with us today as the ranking subcommittee member. She is in Africa.

So we will go to Mr. Brad Sherman, chairman of the Subcommittee on Terrorism, Nonproliferation, and Trade.

Mr. SHERMAN. Boko Haram is but one of many organizations using terror to try to impose a contorted version of 9th Century Islam. It touches our hearts to see the victims from North Africa, through the Middle East, and through South Asia.

But it is also a threat to the United States. Whether these groups claim to be affiliated with al-Qaeda or don't claim the al-Qaeda franchise, whether their chief focus is local and their secondary focus is worldwide Jihad or the reverse, the war against violent extremism is not one that we can declare to be over just because we are tired of it. It has been one of our longest conflicts, exceeded at this point only by the Cold War, but it has to be won. We have to turn off the money to groups like Boko Haram.

And I hope that we will get some testimony as to the Gulf oil, state and other money that is or is not being detected going to these groups.

And we have to provide the military aid to the Nigerian Government and other host governments to deal with this extremism.

I yield back.

Chairman ROYCE. Thank you.

Lastly, we go for 1 minute to Mr. Ted Poe, a former judge and the chair of the Subcommittee on Terrorism, Nonproliferation, and Trade.

Mr. POE. Boko Haram showed the world its evil ways when it arrogantly kidnapped over 200 innocent schoolgirls, threatened to marry them off to their fighters and traffic them out of the country as property and as slaves.

As a judge, I have seen the ills of human trafficking and other despicable acts. And this is the ultimate human rights violation, but it is not a surprise, given who these outlaws are.

Unfortunately, the State Department did not want to designate Boko Haram as a Foreign Terrorist Organization until 14 months after the FBI and other government organizations made their plea to designate the group.

In fact, the State Department didn't make the announcement until the day before my subcommittee held a joint hearing with Mr. Smith's subcommittee on the threat of Boko Haram in mid-November of 2013.

Interesting timing, wouldn't you think? We should have listed Boko Haram earlier. Instead, we worried about diplomatic relations. Nonsense rules the day.

After fighting the FTO designation for so long, I am curious how the State Department has implemented the designation and what, if anything, we are doing to stop this Foreign Terrorist Organization. Do we have a plan? What is the plan?

I yield back.

Chairman ROYCE. We are joined this morning by representatives of the Department of State and the Department of Defense. We welcome them.

Prior to being sworn in earlier this year as Under Secretary of State for Civilian Security, Democracy, and Human Rights, Dr. Sarah Sewall served as a senior lecturer in public policy at the John F. Kennedy School of Government at Harvard University. Dr. Sewall also served as Deputy Assistant Secretary for Peacekeeping and Humanitarian Assistance at the Department of Defense from 1993 to 1996.

Ms. Amanda Dory is the Deputy Assistant Secretary of Defense for African Affairs in the Office of the Secretary of Defense. A career member of the Senior Executive Service, Ms. Dory previously served as Deputy Assistant Secretary of Defense for Strategy. She is a recipient of the Presidential Rank Award for her work on the 2010 Quadrennial Defense Review.

And without objection, the witnesses' full prepared statements will be made part of the record. Members will have 5 calendar days to submit any statements or questions to the witnesses or to submit any extraneous material for the record here.

And we will start with Dr. Sewall. If you would summarize your remarks and hold it to 5 minutes. And then afterwards we will go to questions. Dr. Sewall.

Ms. SEWALL. Thank you very much. Chairman Royce—here we go.

Thank you, Chairman Royce.

Chairman ROYCE. Thank you. Make sure your microphone is on there.

And, also, without objection, I would like to include for the record Ms. Deborah Peter's testimony, which she recounted and gave us this morning, members of this committee who met with her. We are going to make that part of the record. And thank you, Deborah, for that.

All right. Dr. Sewall.

STATEMENT OF THE HONORABLE SARAH SEWALL, UNDER SECRETARY FOR CIVILIAN SECURITY, DEMOCRACY, AND HUMAN RIGHTS, U.S. DEPARTMENT OF STATE

Ms. SEWALL. Chairman Royce, Ranking Member Engel, and members of the committee, thank you for inviting me here today to discuss Nigeria's struggle against Boko Haram, one of the most lethal terrorist groups in Africa today. And thank you, Mr. Chairman and the committee, for your longtime leadership on African issues.

Over a month ago the world was outraged when Boko Haram kidnapped some 250 young women from a secondary school in Chibok, and the United States swiftly joined the effort to help the Government of Nigeria safely recover the hostages. President Obama pledged our full support, and President Goodluck Jonathan readily accepted Secretary Kerry's offer of assistance.

Today in Nigeria's capital, Abuja, a robust multidisciplinary team from the United States Government is working hand in hand with Nigerian counterparts and teams from half a dozen other countries, such as the United Kingdom and France.

Our military and civilian experts in intelligence, military planning, hostage negotiations, strategic communications, civilian protection, and victim support have been given unprecedented access and cooperation to assist Nigeria's effort to safely recover the kidnapped schoolgirls.

This effort, one that would be daunting for any government, will necessarily entail not just a diplomatic approach, but, also, law enforcement and diplomat—not just a military approach, but, also, a law enforcement and diplomatic effort.

During our trip last week, AFRICOM Commander General David Rodriguez and I met with Nigeria's top security officials to stress America's support for Nigerian efforts and to reiterate the need for Nigeria to redouble its efforts to defeat Boko Haram while respecting human rights and ensuring the protection of civilians.

This past weekend Under Secretary of State for Political Affairs, Wendy Sherman, continued America's conversation with Nigerian President Jonathan, heads of state from neighboring countries, and other key partners at a summit in Paris convened by French President Hollande. Coming 1 day after Boko Haram killed and kidnapped Chinese nationals in North Cameroon. The kidnappings underscored why Boko Haram is a regional challenge.

And while the kidnappings have cast a spotlight on this terrorist organization, I want to emphasize that, for roughly a decade, the

United States has been working to help the people of Nigeria and the Nigerian Government address this terrorist threat.

Today I would like to highlight some of the kinds of security assistance that we have more recently been providing to help Nigeria address Boko Haram.

Fiscal years 2012, 2013, Department of State planned approximately $35.8 million in security assistance programs that would benefit Nigeria, subject to congressional notification and approval.

We are working with vetted police and civilian security components to build Nigerian law enforcement capacities to investigate terrorist cases, effectively deal with explosive devices, and secure Nigeria's borders. We do this because the most effective counterterrorism policies and practices are those which respect human rights and are underpinned by the rule of law.

We are also focusing on enabling various Nigerian security services, including the police, intelligence agencies, and the Ministry of Defense, refusing multiple information streams to develop a better understanding of Boko Haram.

We engage in robust dialogue with our Nigerian counterparts on these activities, including through the U.S.-Nigeria Binational Commission's Regional Security Working Group. There is also a lengthy history of DoD involvement, which I will leave to my Defense Department colleague to describe.

The Department has also considered other steps to support the fight against Boko Haram. As you know, its leaders do not have bank accounts and the organization is not structured as many other terrorist organizations against whom the United States has used particular legal designations.

After careful deliberation and consultation with the Nigerian Government, the United States decided in June 2012 to designate Boko Haram's top commanders as specially designated global terrorists, which allowed us to implement an asset freeze, a travel ban, and a prohibition on providing weapons or material support to these designated individuals as relevant.

In June 2013, we decided to add Abubakar—forgive my pronunciation—Shekau, Boko Haram's official leader, to our Rewards for Justice Program with a $7-million reward for information leading to his arrest.

In November 2013, after implementing and assessing these earlier steps and building on our long record of security cooperation, and shortly after Nigeria and the United Kingdom made their own designations, we also designated Boko Haram as a Foreign Terrorist Organization.

Our approach reflected our evolving assessment of Boko Haram's threat potential, the utility of additional sanctions of different types, and our close coordination with our partners.

Significantly, while Nigeria had been reluctant to seek international attention to the Boko Haram crisis, it has now moved forward, in part, at our urging to request that the United Nations Security Council designate Boko Haram under its al-Qaeda regime.

And while these efforts will make a difference, we continue to have concerns that corruption and human rights violations by government forces, particularly those forces that have operated in the northeast, continue to undermine the government's attempts to defeat Boko Haram militarily.

Given these concerns, we continue to press the Government of Nigeria to demonstrate that it is working to protect civilians where Boko Haram is not, and this means ending impunity for human rights violations by security forces.

Let me be clear that there is no equivalence between the actions of the Nigerian military and those of Boko Haram, a terrorist group that seeks to murder civilians in large numbers and terrorize the civilian population as a matter of policy, killing over 1,200 people in 2014 thus far.

Yet, we also know the power of popular grievance narratives against the government, and it's incumbent upon Nigeria's Government to demonstrate through specific steps the will to ensure its forces protect human rights for all of its people and end impunity for those that use violence indiscriminately.

Consistent with our council 2 months ago, the Government of Nigeria announced a multifaceted ''soft'' approach to countering Boko Haram, and we are eager to see it implemented.

And we are also eager to see the Nigerian Government address the underlying concerns that impede their ability to address Boko Haram.

In closing, I will say that the State Department, like the American people, hopes very much to see the Nigerian schoolgirls reunited with their families soon.

But we are also prepared for a long, tough fight to defeat Boko Haram and to help the Nigerian people realize the political and economic potential of their great country.

Thank you.

[The prepared statement of Ms. Sewall follows:]

Testimony of Dr. Sarah Sewall,

Under Secretary of State for Civilian Security, Democracy, and

Human Rights

House Foreign Affairs Committee

"Boko Haram: The Growing Threat to Schoolgirls, Nigeria, and

Beyond"

May 21, 2014

Chairman Royce, Ranking Member Engel, and Members of the Committee, thank you for inviting me to discuss Nigeria's struggle against Boko Haram, one of the most lethal terrorist groups in Africa today.

Over a month ago, the world was shocked when Boko Haram kidnapped over 250 young women from a secondary school in Chibok. The United States swiftly joined the effort to help the Government of Nigeria safely recover the hostages.

President Obama pledged our full support, and President Goodluck Jonathan readily accepted Secretary Kerry's offer of assistance. Today in Nigeria's capital, Abuja, a robust multidisciplinary team from the United States government is working hand in hand with Nigerian counterparts and teams from a half dozen other countries such as the United Kingdom and France. Our military and civilian experts in intelligence, military planning, hostage negotiations, strategic communications, civilian protection, and victim support, have been given unprecedented access and cooperation to assist Nigeria's effort to safely recover the kidnapped schoolgirls. This effort – one that is extremely difficult and, as we know from our own experience, may take far longer than we would like – will necessarily entail not just a military approach, but also law enforcement and diplomatic approaches. This kidnapping – and addressing the threat of Boko Haram more broadly – would be daunting for any government. That is why the United States is doing all it can to help Nigeria address these challenges – today and longer term.

During our trip last week, AFRICOM Commander General David Rodriguez and I met Nigeria's top security officials to stress the importance of resolving this crisis and redoubling the effort to defeat Boko Haram, while respecting human rights and ensuring the protection of civilians. In Paris, Under Secretary for Political Affairs Wendy Sherman continued this conversation with Nigerian President Jonathan and heads of state from neighboring countries at a summit convened by French President Hollande in Paris. The summit brought together President Jonathan with presidents of his four neighbors (Benin, Cameroon, Chad, and Niger) as well as senior representatives of the United States, United Kingdom, and European Union. Coming one day after Boko Haram killed and kidnapped Chinese nationals in northern Cameroon, the summit made clear and urgent for all parties the growing regional dimension of this challenge.

The leaders discussed the safe return of the school girls held hostage, and shared concrete ideas on how to defeat Boko Haram such as improving cooperation on border security, countering violent extremism, and redoubling efforts to promote economic growth and create jobs in the affected region. This is consistent with the comprehensive approach Nigeria announced in March and we have repeatedly called for this broad effort to be implemented.

At the summit, the U.S., United Kingdom, and France established a coordination mechanism at various levels to ensure our development, diplomatic, and security assistance are synchronized, including with our African partners. We again called on our African partners to establish national CT strategies, to integrate them across the region, and to share them with P3 and other partners. The United States has worked with Nigeria to impose UN Security Council sanctions on Boko Haram, which we expect to be completed this week.

Peace and security in Nigeria is one of our highest foreign policy priorities in Africa. The tragedy of this kidnapping has rightfully focused our attention on the need to return these girls to their families, and on Boko Haram's increasingly brazen assaults on youth seeking education. Ensuring that girls and boys alike have the opportunity to learn is essential to ensuring that all of Nigeria's people contribute to and benefit from its economic prosperity. As the First Lady recently observed, stories like those of the kidnapped girls – and others who have risked their lives to pursue an education – should serve as a call to action to help the millions of girls worldwide who are not in school.

The kidnappings have also exposed the long-term security challenges that confront Nigeria, one of our most important partners in Africa. The fight against Boko Haram requires more than just military action, it requires a comprehensive approach to improving the lives of people in Northeast Nigeria. Just as my portfolio at the State Department includes counterterrorism, law enforcement, democracy promotion, human rights, conflict response, criminal justice, refugees, trafficking in persons, and religious freedom, Nigeria needs to address all of these important, inter-related issues in its fight against Boko Haram. Nigeria is not only a critical regional political and economic leader, but also a partner with which we work closely together in multilateral fora, including the UN Security Council.

While the kidnapping in Chibok has cast a spotlight on Boko Haram, I want to emphasize that we have *long* been working to help the people of Nigeria and the Nigerian government address this terrorist threat. Boko Haram is a Nigerian-based group that became considerably more violent in 2009 and has metastasized into a regional threat. It is responsible for the brutal killing of thousands of people in Nigeria, resulting in over 1000 deaths and injuries in 2013 alone. Boko Haram also operates in Cameroon's Far North Region and the Lake Chad Basin and has kidnapped high-profile Westerners and, just recently, Chinese nationals in Cameroon. While we are rightfully focused on the almost 300 girls who were kidnapped, this tragedy is not an isolated incident. Going back just a few months, in February, over 59 teenage boys were killed in an attack, and, earlier this month, Boko Haram carried out an attack on two towns, killing an estimated 300 people.

As we pursue an integrated approach to helping Nigeria meet its challenges, we want Nigeria to prevail in its efforts, which we believe can only be accomplished through a comprehensive, whole-of-government approach to defeating Boko Haram. We know from experience the difficulty in confronting an enemy that knows no borders and kills civilians indiscriminately. The most urgent need we see today is for Nigerian forces to conduct intelligence-driven operations that avoid civilian casualties, in order to help enhance trust and cooperation with northern populations and expose the relatively small numbers of Boko Haram fighters. More broadly, Nigeria's approach in the Northeast should emphasize and inspire respect for human rights, rule of law and accountability, and development and responsive governance. We are seeing small measures of slow progress, including the Nigerian government's announcement two months ago of a multi-faceted "soft" approach to Boko Haram. We are eager to see and to help Nigeria now implement this plan and have offered assistance to that end, including sharing our own lessons learned in how to effectively carry out counterterrorism operations while ensuring the protection of civilians.

Today, I would like to highlight some of the kinds of security assistance that we have been providing to help Nigeria address Boko Haram. A fuller description of our counterterrorism assistance to Nigeria can be found in the Fact Sheet about Boko Haram and U.S. Counterterrorism Assistance to Nigeria released by the State Department on May 14. In Fiscal Years 2012 and 2013, the Department of State planned approximately $35.8 million in security assistance programs that benefit Nigeria, subject to Congressional notification and approval.

Our security assistance reflects our efforts to ensure Nigeria takes a comprehensive approach to countering Boko Haram. We are working with vetted police and civilian security components to build Nigerian law enforcement capacities to investigate terrorism cases, effectively deal with explosive devices, and secure Nigeria's borders. We do this because the most effective counterterrorism policies and practices are those that respect human rights and are underpinned by the rule of law. For example, our West African Regional Security Initiative provided nearly $3.7 million in assistance to the Nigerian Economic and Financial Crimes Commission in Fiscal Year 2013 to help Nigeria counter corruption, money laundering, and terrorist financing, and help reform the police and promote the rule of law. We are also focused on enabling various Nigerian security services, including the police, various intelligence agencies, and the ministry of defense, with fusing multiple information streams to develop a better understanding of Boko Haram. My DOD colleague will speak to this more fully, but our military assistance supports the professionalization of vetted military units and improves their ability to plan and implement appropriate steps to counter Boko Haram and ensure civilian security. We have a robust dialogue with our Nigerian counterparts on all of these efforts, including through the U.S.-Nigeria Binational Commission's Regional Security Working Group.

While these efforts will make a difference, we continue to have concerns that human rights violations by government forces – particularly those forces that have operated in the Northeast – are undermining the government's attempts to defeat Boko Haram. Given these concerns, we continue to press the Government of Nigeria to demonstrate that it is working to protect civilians where Boko Haram is not—this means ending impunity for human rights violations by security forces. For example, alongside the Nigerian people and their own human rights commission, as well as Amnesty International and others, we have asked the Government to investigate massacres allegedly committed by government security forces that occurred in the village of Baga in April 2013 and at the Giwa Barracks detention facility after

Boko Haram staged a prison break there in March of this year. Only with facts uncovered and perpetrators brought to justice can the Nigerian government demonstrate that it is working to preserve life and fairly administer justice.

Let me be clear that there is no equivalence between the actions of the Nigerian military and those of Boko Haram, a terrorist group which has made clear that it is seeking to murder civilians in large numbers and terrorize the civilian population as a matter of policy. Yet, we also know the power of popular grievance narratives against governments, and it is incumbent on Nigeria's government to demonstrate through specific steps the will to ensure its forces protect the human rights of all of its people and end impunity for those that use violence indiscriminately. Civilians in the Northeast must be assured that security services are there to protect them from Boko Haram's violence. The confidence and cooperation of civilians is critical to deny Boko Haram a safe haven and gather the intelligence necessary to, among other pressing goals, safely recover the girls kidnapped at Chibok. Moreover, when military and security forces are found to commit human rights violations and the government does not act to hold the perpetrators of these incidents responsible for their actions, we are then limited as a matter of U.S law and policy to work with units involved in these incidents. We are eager to help the Nigerian government address these concerns, which impede our ability to help in preventing punishing, and rectifying Boko Haram's atrocities.

Let me say a few words about how the provisions of law concerning security assistance and human rights known as the "Leahy laws" affect our work to assist the Nigerian government combat Boko Haram. Let me be clear: We value and strongly support the tenets and purpose behind the Leahy laws, and we have worked within U.S. law and policy to assist the Nigerians in their fight against Boko Haram. There is no question that the behavior of certain Nigerian military actors have made it impossible for the United States to work directly with them. To better understand the possibilities of promoting change, I will ensure that we are working to the greatest extent possible to build Nigeria's capacity as a rights-respecting security partner and to encourage the reform of its military to more effectively address the Boko Haram threat.

In addition, pervasive corruption undermines the government's fight against Boko Haram. The Nigerian government has one of sub-Saharan Africa's largest security budgets, with $5.8 billion dedicated to security in its proposed 2014 budget. Yet corruption prevents supplies as basic as bullets and transport vehicles from reaching the front lines of the struggle against Boko Haram. Morale is low and desertions are common among soldiers in Nigeria's 7th Army Division. For example, on May 14, 7th Division soldiers reportedly fired at their commander's car, complaining that he had failed to ensure they received the necessary equipment. As this incident shows, Nigeria will need to seriously tackle corruption if it is to succeed in stamping out Boko Haram.

These challenges are even more acute in the lead up to February 2015, when Nigeria will hold its fifth presidential election since its return to democracy in 1999. The last election, held in 2011, showed improvements in election administration, but was followed by riots that claimed over 800 lives, mostly in northern states. Insecurity and political tensions have fueled fears that 2015 may see even greater violence.

We are of course concerned about the northeast, where Boko Haram operates, and where it will be critical for the government to ensure security so that Nigerians in the Northeast are able to vote, including in three states of emergency. We are also working to help address instability in Nigeria's Middle Belt, where complex conflicts over land have pitted communities against one another, and the Niger Delta, where tensions over the allocation of oil revenues remain high and a long-running insurgency is yet to be fully settled. As Nigerians prepare to vote against this backdrop of corruption, tension, and uncertainty, we must look at more than the kidnapping at Chibok to understand and help Nigeria address the full range of challenges to its future.

We are therefore working in other ways to help Nigeria keep civilians safe and strengthen democracy. For example, we are reviewing ways to establish a community-based early warning response to combat GBV in Nigeria, and particularly in the north. We are striving to promote interreligious tolerance in the Middle Belt, and we have an initiative championing narratives of non-violence in the Niger Delta led by local Nigerian community, business, cultural, and economic leaders, and aimed at giving local populations' a voice to promote peace through media. As the 2015 elections approach, our diplomatic engagements are supporting USAID's elections assistance package, which will help the Independent National Electoral Commission, or INEC, to register voters, conduct elections, and run a nationwide voter education campaign to ensure that all citizens understand their rights and know how to exercise them. During my trip to Nigeria, I met INEC Chairman Professor Attahiru Jega to discuss preparations for the elections, the status of northeastern states' ability to participate in elections, and convey our interest in the credibility and peacefulness of the vote. We continue to call on all political parties and candidates to publicly renounce violence and commit to ensuring a free, fair, and peaceful election.

Before I close, I would like to address two aspects of the State Department's approach toward Nigeria and Boko Haram. The first concerns the timing of the designation of Boko Haram as a Foreign Terrorist Organization. While I was not at the State Department at that time, the Department pursued the designation after careful deliberation and consultation with the Nigerian government and after a series of steps that included our June 2012 designation of Boko Haram's top commanders as Specially Designated Global Terrorists and our June 2013 decision to add Abubakar Shekau, Boko Haram's official leader to our Rewards for Justice Program. We made the FTO designation after implementing and assessing these earlier steps, and shortly after Nigeria and the United Kingdom made their own designations. In short, our approach to the FTO designation reflected our evolving assessment of Boko Haram's threat potential, the utility of additional sanctions available pursuant to FTO designation, and our close coordination with our partners. Significantly, while Nigeria has been reluctant to seek international attention to the Boko Haram crisis, it has moved forward this month, in part at our urging, to request that the United Nations Security Council designate Boko Haram under its al Qa'ida sanctions regime.

The second issue concerns whether Boko Haram, and particularly the kidnapping at Chibok, is part of a worldwide trend of persecutions against Christians. We are committed to protecting the rights of people of all religions, including Christians, to practice their beliefs freely and peacefully. Certainly Boko Haram has targeted Christians, and Nigerian officials believe that 85% of the girls kidnapped at Chibok are Christians and have been forced to convert to Islam after their kidnapping. We want to highlight, however, that Boko Haram is a problem that affects Nigerians of every religion. Indeed, the majority of Boko Haram's estimated 4,000 total victims to date have been Muslim. Even as we work to help the Government of Nigeria protect Christians, we are also helping it protect its population as a whole. In the aftermath of the kidnappings, we have encouraged Muslim and Christian faith leaders alike to speak out, in Nigeria and around the world, to urge respect for religious diversity and interfaith cooperation. I can assure you that we treat issues of religious freedom, like other issues of universal human rights and fundamental freedoms, with utmost seriousness.

The State Department, like the American people, hope to see the girls reunited with their families soon. But we are also preparing for a long, tough fight to defeat Boko Haram and to help the Nigerian people – including Nigeria's girls and boys alike – realize the full political and economic potential of their great country.

––––––––––

Chairman ROYCE. Ms. Dory.

STATEMENT OF MS. AMANDA J. DORY, DEPUTY ASSISTANT SECRETARY OF DEFENSE FOR AFRICAN AFFAIRS, U.S. DEPARTMENT OF DEFENSE

Ms. DORY. Good morning, Chairman Royce, Ranking Member Engel, members of the committee.

Thank you for calling us together to address the deeply disturbing abductions of more than 270 schoolgirls from Northern Nigeria by the terrorist organization Boko Haram some 5 weeks ago. The global community has been horrified by this barbarous act.

Within the context of the U.S. Government response, the Department of Defense is taking action to help the Nigerian authority's efforts to recover the girls safely and address the growing threat of Boko Haram.

Sixteen DoD personnel from multiple locations have joined the multidisciplinary team of experts led by the State Department at our Embassy in Abuja.

Their initial efforts have been to work with Nigerian security personnel to identify gaps and shortfalls and provide requested expertise and information, including the use of intelligence, surveillance, and reconnaissance support.

We are also working closely with the U.K., France, and other international partners in Abuja to coordinate multilateral actions.

Our intent is to support Nigerian-led efforts to safely recover the girls and help catalyze greater efforts to secure the population of Nigeria from the menace of Boko Haram.

To be clear, immediate and long-term solutions to Boko Haram must be developed and implemented by the sovereign Government of Nigeria if sustained security is to be achieved.

Extant in its current form since 2009, the Boko Haram threat has grown over the past several years, extending its geographic reach and increasing the sophistication and lethality of its attacks.

Along with other U.S. departments and agencies, DoD has been engaging for some time with the Government of Nigeria to help build its capacity to respond.

Beginning in January 2011, we have used the State Department-led U.S.-Nigeria Binational Commission as our principal forum to tackle the challenge of enhancing counterinsurgency efforts while developing a civilian-centered approach to security that is comprehensive, engaging law enforcement, border security, as well as the underlying contributors to instability, such as governance, education, health, and economic development.

For its part, DoD is supporting the establishment of counter-IED and civil-military operations capacity within the Nigerian Army as part of Nigeria's security doctrine.

We have also supported the establishment of a national-level intelligence fusion capability to promote better information sharing among the various Nigerian national security entities.

Most recently, in late April of this year, we began working with Nigeria's newly created counterterrorism-focused Ranger Battalion.

As has been demonstrated recently, Boko Haram uses the lightly controlled borders between Nigeria and its neighbors for cross-border operations.

Last week, France hosted a very timely summit at which heads of state from Nigeria, Chad, Cameroon, Benin, Niger, along with the U.S. and U.K., sought to improve regional collaboration.

For our part, DoD and the Department of State are working closely together on a proposal to enhance border security along Nigeria's common borders with Chad, Niger, and Cameroon in support of a regional response to counter the threat posed by Boko Haram.

The concept is to build border security capacity and promote better cooperation and communication among the security forces of each country with the aim of reducing Boko Haram's operational space and safe havens.

As committed as the U.S. is to supporting Nigeria and in returning these girls safely, Nigeria's fight against Boko Haram is a very challenging case. In the face of a new and more sophisticated threat, Nigeria's security forces have been greatly challenged by Boko Haram's tactics.

Also troubling have been the heavy-handed approaches by security forces during operations against Boko Haram, approaches that risk further alienating local populations.

Consistent with U.S. law and policy, we review all security units nominated for assistance, and we do not provide assistance when there is credible information of human rights violations. With this important consideration in mind, we have worked to engage where we are able.

No discussion of how to address Boko Haram would be complete without addressing some of the political dynamics in Nigeria and the underlying security environment.

In spite of its vast oil wealth, Nigeria continues to face enormous development challenges. When these factors are combined with pervasive corruption and Boko Haram's brutal terrorization of the population, Northern Nigerians lack a reliable source of security.

The long-term solution to Boko Haram cannot come solely from Nigeria's security forces, but, rather, also requires Nigeria's political leaders to give serious and sustained attention to addressing the systematic problems of corruption, the lack of effective and equitable governance, and the country's uneven social and economic development.

While continuing to draw attention to these broader factors, we will remain sharply focused on the heartwrenching event that triggered this broader awareness of Boko Haram's depredations.

DoD is committed to supporting Nigeria's efforts to locate and recover these girls. This will not be an easy task, as hostage recovery is a high-risk undertaking in the best of circumstances.

If this terrible episode is to resolve with the girls' safe returns, the Government of Nigeria must continue to match its public statements with a serious and focused response that draws on all elements of its government, the influence of key social and religious figures, and the resources international partners are making available to assist.

Thank you.

Chairman ROYCE. Well, thank you for that testimony.

[The prepared statement of Ms. Dory follows:]

House Committee on Foreign Affairs

"Boko Haram: The Growing Threat to Schoolgirls, Nigeria, and Beyond "

Testimony of Amanda Dory
Deputy Assistant Secretary of Defense for African Affairs

Chairman Royce, Ranking Member Engel, thank you for calling us together to address the deeply disturbing abductions of over 270 school girls in northern Nigeria by the terrorist organization Boko Haram some five weeks ago. The global community has been horrified by this barbarous act. Within the context of the U.S. government response, the Department of Defense is taking action to help the Nigerian authorities' efforts to recover the girls safely and address the growing threat from Boko Haram.

On Friday, May 9th, the DoD directed sixteen personnel from multiple locations to our embassy in Abuja to join a multi-disciplinary team of experts led by our Department of State. Their specialties include medical, intelligence, counter-terrorism and communications expertise and their mission is to support U.S. Ambassador Jim Entwistle and the State-Department's team led by Mike Hoza. The DoD team members' initial efforts have been to work with Nigerian security personnel to analyze Nigerian operations, identify gaps and shortfalls, and otherwise provide requested expertise and information to the Nigerian authorities, including through the use of intelligence, surveillance, and reconnaissance support. We are also working closely with the UK, France, and other international partners in Abuja to coordinate multilateral actions in order to maximize our collective assistance efforts.

Our intent is to support Nigerian-led efforts to safely recover the girls and help catalyze greater efforts to secure the population of northern Nigeria from the menace of Boko Haram. To be clear, immediate and long-term solutions to the current threat that Boko Haram poses to the people of Nigeria must be developed and implemented by the sovereign government of Nigeria if sustained security is to be achieved.

Extant in its current form since 2009, the threat to Nigeria from Boko Haram has grown over the past several years, extending its geographic reach and increasing the sophistication and lethality of its attacks. Multiple dramatic recent attacks – including its extremely damaging strike on a Nigerian air base, as well as the coordinated, methodical and highly successful attack at the Giwa barracks in Maiduguri – have demonstrated that Boko Haram is now capable of directly and successfully engaging Nigeria's armed forces. Its expanded geographic reach within Nigeria was also tragically demonstrated in an attack on the UN headquarters in August of 2011, and when over 70 innocent Nigerian citizens were killed in a vehicle-borne IED attack just outside the national capital of Abuja on the same day as the kidnapping of the girls in Chibok.

In fact, the kidnapping in Chibok was only the most recent outrage in a growing portfolio of Boko Haram assaults on education, the civilian population, and the government of Nigeria. Other attacks directed against students and teachers in the last year include one on June 16-17, 2013, when nine people were killed in a Boko Haram attack on the Government Secondary School in Damaturu, Yobe state. This was followed on July 6, 2013 by an attack on the secondary school in Mamudo village, in which 29 students were killed, including reports that some were burned alive when their dormitory was deliberately set on fire. On September 28-29, 2013, more than 40 students were slaughtered in a nighttime attack by Boko Haram on the Yobe State College of Agriculture. And in yet another nighttime attack, this time at the Buni Yadi Federal Government College on February 18, 2014, at least 59 people, including boys ranging in age from 11 to 18, were killed.

Along with other U.S. departments and agencies, DoD has been engaging for some time with the government of Nigeria to help it build its own capacity to respond to Boko Haram's growing capabilities. Beginning in January 2011, and most recently in August 2013, we have used the State Department-led U.S.-Nigeria Binational Commission's Regional Security Working Group as our principal forum to tackle the challenge of enhancing counterinsurgency efforts while developing a civilian-centered approach to security. In addition, Nigeria is a member of the 11 country Trans-Sahara Counterterrorism Partnership – TSCTP – along with Cameroon, Chad and Niger. U.S. assistance either bilaterally with Nigeria or in partnership with other TSCTP members is comprehensive and includes engaging law enforcement and border security personnel, as well as addressing the underlying contributors to Nigeria's instability such as governance, education, health, and economic development. For its part, DoD has undertaken a number of initiatives. For example, we are supporting the establishment of counter-IED and civil-military operations capacity within the Nigerian army in order to make C-IED and CMO an integral part of Nigeria's security doctrine. The concept is to develop Nigerian institutions with organic C-IED and CMO skills that can be maintained and passed along by the Nigerians themselves. We have also supported the establishment of a national-level intelligence fusion center in an effort to promote information sharing among various national security entities and, overall, to enable more effective and responsible intelligence-driven CT operations. Most recently, in late April 2014 we began working with Nigeria's newly-created counterterrorism-focused Ranger Battalion to impart the skills and disciplines needed to mount effective operations against Boko Haram. The Nigerian Navy's Special Boat Service (SBS) has been a committed, professional, and enthusiastic partner with which DoD and UK trainers have engaged for several years to build Nigeria's maritime and riverine security capacity thus addressing a different but also-serious threat to Nigeria's security.

As has been demonstrated during recent Boko Haram movements and attacks, Boko Haram uses the relatively lightly controlled borders between Nigeria and its neighbors for cross-border operations in the region. On May 17th, French President Holland hosted a timely Summit in Paris at which heads of state from Nigeria, Chad, Cameroon, Benin, and Niger, along with the U.S., UK and, of course, France, discussed how to achieve a more effective response, including promoting regional collaboration. For our part, DoD and the Department of State are working closely together to develop under the Global Security Contingency Fund – GSCF – authority a proposal to enhance border security along Nigeria's common borders with TSCTP partners Chad, Niger, and Cameroon, in support of a regional response to counter the threat posed by Boko Haram and other illegal actors. The concept is to build border security capacity with, and promote better cooperation and communication among, the security forces of each country. In some cases, assistance would go to the military, in others the gendarmerie, and in still other border security forces, to most effectively detect and respond to the movement of Boko Haram members back and forth among safe havens in Nigeria and neighboring countries. If we can build these basic but critical capacities, progress can be made toward reducing Boko Haram's operational reach from safe havens, halting its spread, and reversing some of the gains it has made.

As committed as the U.S. is to supporting Nigeria in its fight against Boko Haram and in returning these girls safely to their families, Nigeria's fight against this barbaric group is a challenging case. In the face of a new and more sophisticated threat than it has dealt with before, Nigeria's security forces have been greatly challenged by Boko Haram's tactics. Also troubling have been the heavy-handed approaches by Nigerian forces during operations against Boko

Haram – approaches that risk further harming and alienating local populations. Consistent with

U.S. law and policy, we review all security force units nominated for assistance, and we do not

provide assistance when we have credible information that they have committed gross violations

of human rights. With this important consideration in mind, we have worked to engage where

we are able including, by providing training on human rights and law of armed conflict in our

engagements. We have also emphasized the importance of a comprehensive counterinsurgency

approach that includes civil-military operations, protection of civilians, and provision of basic

services, and more broadly, working to convey lessons that we ourselves have spent so much

blood and treasure as a nation developing over the past decade engaging terrorists and

insurgents.

No discussion of how to address the Boko Haram threat would be complete without

addressing some of the political dynamics in Nigeria and the underlying security environment.

In spite of its vast oil wealth, Nigeria continues to face enormous development challenges.

When these factors are combined with pervasive corruption and Boko Haram's brutal

terrorization of the population, northern Nigerians are left without a reliable source of security.

The long-term solution to Boko Haram cannot come solely from Nigeria's military or security

forces, but rather also requires Nigeria's political leaders to give serious and sustained attention

to addressing the systemic problems of corruption, the lack of effective and equitable

governance, and the country's uneven social and economic development.

While we work to address these broader factors, we will also remain sharply focused on

the heart wrenching event that has brought us here today. The tragic situation of these girls and the families who hope for their safe return has captured the attention of the world. As I have highlighted already, DoD is committed to supporting Nigeria's efforts to locate and recover these girls. This will not be an easy task, as hostage recovery is a high-risk undertaking in the best of circumstances. We are still seeking information on whether and how the girls may have been dispersed. Indeed, if this terrible episode is to resolve with the girls' safe return, the government of Nigeria must continue to match its public statements with a serious and focused response that draws on all elements of its government, the influence of key social and religious figures, and the resources international partners are making available to assist.

Chairman ROYCE. As you testified, you do not provide assistance when human rights violations occur. However, there is a provision whereby, in an extraordinary circumstance, we could.

And here is the argument that I would make about Boko Haram and why this is an extraordinary circumstance. You have a situation here where we are focused on the kidnapping of 300 girls some weeks ago, but, in the meantime, more have been kidnapped.

As we talk about it, an additional group of schoolgirls were kidnapped. As we talk about it, additional attacks have occurred, 118 killed this morning, you know, 300 killed a few weeks ago.

As we talk about it, 500 schools have been destroyed, and Boko Haram—their modus operandi is to destroy the schools and then recruit young uneducated men into their ranks and teach them Jihad.

And so, as the Jihad mushrooms out across North Africa and into Cameroon and into Chad and into neighboring states, we say, "Well, you know, human rights violations have occurred in Nigeria; so, we are limited in what we can do."

The difficulty is that Boko Haram is in a process of expanding their terror and the frequency of these attacks, the attacks on girls, that has been an evolution.

They have intimidated and frightened the Nigerian military, they are now to the point where a lot of military units have run away. And so they can go in and take girls and then, you know, they can turn them into concubines or sell them or, you know, enslave them, because that is what they are actually doing. They are enslaving.

And I would say that is an extraordinary circumstance that might necessitate the U.S. We have U.S. forces well positioned to advise and assist Nigerian forces in the search for these girls and, in this role, U.S. forces are trained to deal with hostage situations. Unfortunately, the Nigerian forces are not. They are trained to deal and track in jungle environments.

They can advise and assist right up to the point of an attack. They don't have to be involved in the attack. But they could use those unique assets that the U.S. has in terms of our spy satellite capabilities and et cetera in order to track and rescue these girls.

This would be very similar to the mission that we have approved with respect to the Lord's Resistance Army. And for a number of years, if you think about it—how many years did it take us to galvanize some support against Joseph Kony?

I think it was about 15 years of Joseph Kony marauding and kidnapping young boys and making child soldiers out of 12-year-old boys and young girls and making them concubines. I think 15,000 was roughly the number of people he slaughtered before we finally put him on defense by authorizing U.S. forces to help track him.

So now he is the one that is being tracked instead of the one tracking others. Right? It used to be he would maraud—he would take his band into Congo or Northern Uganda or Southern Sudan or Central African Republic and just create mayhem.

But now at least he is on the run. Somebody said this morning, "Well, we haven't got him yet." No. We haven't caught him yet, but he is on the run. And there is little doubt that they are going to run him down, and it is a completely different situation than it was a couple of years ago when he was on the offensive.

Now, you have got the same situation here. And, frankly, we should do the same thing. For the sake of humanity, we should do the same thing. We should not allow this cancer to spread the way it has.

We heard from Deborah this morning—Deborah Peter—about the uncompromising position where they tell her father, you know, that he has to quit. He was a pastor.

You know, they burned the church, they killed him, they killed her young brother, and now they have kidnapped her schoolmates. I think the time is at hand for the United States to help build the morale.

Think about what this would mean to the Nigerian forces if we were willing to give them this assistance. You could ensure that the strategy for the rescue operation launched by them is very well planned.

You could boost the morale and effectiveness of the Nigerian forces, and you could ensure that our intelligence, reconnaissance, and surveillance assets are put to best use.

So I would just ask for your response, if you could, to the observation. Is there any reason why we can't offer that waiver and treat this the same way we have treated going after Joseph Kony?

Ms. DORY. I think the waiver issue I would defer to my State Department colleague in terms of the specific provisions of Leahy.

But what I could quickly do is agree in terms of some of the diagnostics as you look at the situation with the Lord's Resistance Army and why we are on a successful path collectively at this point, and how that pertains to the Boko Haram situation.

You have identified, Congressman, the elements of success. You have neighbors who are working together under a regional task force construct to address the LRA challenge.

You have a Ugandan Government dedicated to addressing the governance and the economic concerns of Northern Uganda, which helps give rise to the phenomenon of the Lord's Resistance Army in the first place.

With external support, Uganda and the other forces have been able to develop an intelligence and information picture that has been very important and then launched a very successful information campaign that reaches the populations in the affected areas that are then able to further assist in the tracking operations.

So I think many of those elements are very relevant to how we could productively work with Nigeria and its neighbors going forward vis-à-vis Boko Haram.

Chairman ROYCE. And, Ms. Dory, I would just add one other thing for your consideration.

And maybe Dr. Sewall would like to comment on this as well.

But the one difference is that, with Boko Haram, we have a group that is a threat to U.S. interests as well, to quote the State Department testimony over on the Senate side, or perhaps it was the Defense Department.

But there is no question that a Jihadist group like this, that directs its efforts and its bombing against those who believe in empowering women or teaching women, is also a threat to the United States and our interests.

So it would seem to me that, if we are going to authorize this with respect to going after Joseph Kony, we certainly should do it here.

Dr. Sewall?

Ms. SEWALL. Thank you for your observations. And I share your sense of urgency about the matter.

I think, with respect to the specific question concerning sanctions, it is my understanding that there is limited waiver authority in the case of national security emergencies and that the decision rests at the highest levels of the government with regard to exercising a national security emergency exception.

Chairman ROYCE. Is it under consideration as an exemption?

Ms. SEWALL. I can't speak to what the senior members of this government are discussing with regard to Leahy. I think the focus right now is very much on the safe rescue of the girls. And so, when I——

Chairman ROYCE. Yes. But the Leahy Amendment is what prohibits our active cooperation. In the steps that I just enumerated here, you know, in the tracking on the ground and to be able to plan that attack on the ground, that is the whole point.

I mean, we had the testimony by the Defense Department last week in the Senate that, "This vetting is a persistent and very troubling limitation on our ability to provide assistance"—they are talking about the Leahy provision here—"particularly training assistance that the Nigerians so badly need." So this is a problem.

Ms. SEWALL. And so I would like to address it.

The issue is to disaggregate the immediate crisis and what options are available to deal with supporting the Nigerians in their effort to rescue the girls versus longer-term systemic and force-wide engagement.

And I think it is very important to both disaggregate those and then to look at the facts as they pertain to each case.

In the first case, I spoke yesterday to the deployment team in Abuja, and they are very pleased with the growing level of cooperation that exists, both within the Intel Fusion Center and with their broader discussions with their Nigerian counterparts.

They are hopeful that U.S. assistance will be increasingly useful to the Nigerians in their effort, and they, nonetheless, rely on choices made by the Government of Nigeria in terms of what they would like to avail themselves of and how to proceed.

More broadly, the security systems issue—and, again, I think Amanda Dory can speak in great detail about the level of security assistance that is occurring right now.

But we have been able to, pursuant to the Leahy Law, create essentially two new battalions with whom we are working—one is specialized counterterrorism force, and the other a Ranger Battalion to create their specialized military capabilities with regard to the kind of military challenges that Boko Haram presents.

Chairman ROYCE. Here would be my suggestion. Thank you. Here is my suggestion. Ask for a temporary waiver. If you don't want the permanent waiver, ask for a temporary waiver, designate this as an extraordinary circumstance, and get to an answer to the point that your colleague made from the Department of Defense that it is a ''persistent and very troubling limitation on our ability to provide assistance, particularly training assistance, that the Nigerians so badly need.'' That is the statement from the Department of Defense. It needs to be addressed.

But I need to go to Mr. Engel. My time has long since expired. Mr. Engel.

Mr. ENGEL. Thank you. Thank you very much, Mr. Chairman.

I was in favor of declaring Boko Haram as a terrorist organization, but I want to address the undercurrent with some of my friends on the other side of the aisle that somehow the lack of designating them as a terrorist organization earlier contributed somehow to this kidnapping. I think that is absurd.

You know, when the State Department didn't designate Boko Haram as an FTO, it wasn't because anyone was being careless. It wasn't because they weren't paying attention. It was a policy decision based on facts on the ground.

Facts changed and the Department issued a designation. It is not clear what the designation does—asset freezes and Visa bans and prohibition of material support—that that has actually made a difference.

But, you know, designating Boko Haram as an FTO earlier would have helped the organization's fundraising and recruiting efforts. Organizations like Boko Haram aren't afraid of being branded terrorists by the U.S. That word is a badge of honor.

I am also told that the Nigerian Government didn't want the designation. That is the reason the State Department didn't issue it.

And in May 2012, 25 leading experts on Nigeria wrote the State Department, saying that an FTO designation for Boko Haram was a bad idea.

And in 2012, the State Department did designate the top three leaders of Boko Haram as specially designated nationals, which are terrorists, meaning that we could go after them and their network.

And, in fact, Secretary Clinton visited Nigeria in 2012 to consult with the Nigerian Government on how we could work together.

So while I have been in favor of declaring them as a terrorist organization, I don't think anyone can seriously think that, if we had done it earlier, it would have somehow prevented this kidnapping.

So I would like either Dr. Sewall or Ms. Dory to comment on what I have just said.

Ms. DORY. Congressman—Ranking Member Engel, I think it is fair to say that we work closely with host nation governments regardless of the designation issue. Boko Haram has certainly been on the radar screen in terms of the type of security cooperation that has been effective with Nigeria since it emerged in the Nigerian context years ago.

So the point about the formal designation, it brings some additional tools to bear. Principally, in the financial domain, you mentioned the Visa bans as well. So it can be helpful from that perspective. But it does escalate, in a sense, and that can be why, when engaging with host nations, they may be reluctant to have such an international designation because it draws more attention to the problem, potentially, in unproductive ways.

So I think that is making a linkage to at what point did the designation occur and the practical engagement that has been underway with the Nigerians are really separate issues.

Ms. SEWALL. I think the key point is the extent to which sanctions actually achieve their objectives.

And I think one of the reasons why the administration decided in June 2012 to designate the three top commanders of Boko Haram as specially designated terrorists was because most of the tools that would be available against Boko Haram, as an organization, were then available to use against those three recognized leaders.

The Rewards for Justice Program was an additional effort to find ways to put pressure on the organization. And what fundamentally changed in the context of the FTO designation that followed both of those actions was the ability to take action against the group as opposed to its three top leaders.

So I think it is in that context that it is very important to look at the evolution of U.S. actions, and the primary significance, I think, was in the June 2012 designation of the three Boko Haram top leaders as specially designated terrorists.

Thank you.

Mr. ENGEL. Thank you.

Let me ask you both this: Given the enormous domestic and international attention following these kidnappings, has the Nigerian Government—I said some of it in my opening remarks, and, Ms. Dory, you mentioned it as well—has the Nigerian Government become more receptive to our messages, urging them to change their approach to Boko Haram? And what concrete things have they done to shift their strategy and their relationship with us?

Ms. DORY. I believe the quick answer is "yes." The intensity of international public opinion and support is productively contributing to our dialogue with the Government of Nigeria.

I think their willingness to accept the multidisciplinary team and their robust engagement with it since its arrival are the most concrete indicators in the near term.

Ms. SEWALL. In my recent visit with AFRICOM Commander David Rodriguez, we stressed both of the points that you referenced, both the need to take rapid action to rescue the girls and the need to fundamentally rethink their approach to counterinsurgency.

We talked a lot about the evolution of the U.S. approach to counterinsurgency and the ways in which it is critical to think of a holistic approach, the ways in which a careful approach to violence is absolutely vital for attaining the cooperation and, therefore, the intelligence from the local population, one of the main hindrances in the fight against Boko Haram thus far.

And we also spoke frankly about our concerns about the inability of a seemingly very large defense budget to translate into the receipt of bullets and workable trucks at the level of the 7th Division in the northeast.

Mr. ENGEL. Does the State Department have an estimate of how many people the Nigerian security forces have killed over the last 4 years in Northern Nigeria?

Ms. SEWALL. We do not have an estimate.

But I will tell you that, given my own background as someone who urged the United States Government to count civilian casualties during its counterinsurgency campaigns, this was an issue that I raised repeatedly with all four of the military officials with whom we met.

And my strong advice to them was that they would be unable to evaluate and reform their efforts to protect civilians and to more directly avoid killing civilians by mistake unless they very carefully tracked those casualties.

So it is my hope that, going forward, we will be able to see progress in that regard.

Mr. ENGEL. The chairman and I agree on what we in the United States must do in order to help bring these girls back in terms of working with other countries and forces.

Could you outline for us what are some of the operational challenges to finding and rescuing these girls.

Ms. DORY. Thank you.

The operational challenges are significant. You have seen some of the comparisons in terms of the vastness of the terrain in which the girls may be located.

We are working with our Nigerian counterparts and other international partners to develop a better understanding of where they may be, but our sense at this point is that they have been dispersed into multiple smaller groups. They may or may not all be in Nigeria.

So the sheer number of individuals involved, the complexity of the terrain—jungle for a great part of it—and the movement that could be associated over the weeks that have elapsed, creating a greater area of operations, make this a very difficult environment in which to contemplate what a recovery might look like.

Just to give an example, if you think back to the hostage incident in Amnas, Algeria 2 years ago, where you had 800 hostages who were in a single location and the Algerian Government and military took action as the AQIM and Mokhtar Belmokhtar began to separate and disperse the hostages, they engaged in an assault that left 40 of the hostages dead, and that was in a desert environment and the hostages were all concentrated together.

So it would be hard to overestimate the complexity, first, of locating the hostages and then in considering how that might be resolved successfully.

If we had an FBI witness here today, he or she, I imagine, would indicate that the vast majority of hostage recovery situations are resolved through dialogue and negotiations and not through rescues and assaults.

Mr. ENGEL. Thank you.

Anything to add, Dr. Sewall?

Ms. SEWALL. I think any military experts in hostage recovery would also tell you that a dialogue is often very helpful even in the event that dialogue fails.

And so I think we have to be respectful of the ways in which the Nigerians may choose to try to achieve the safe return of the girls.

Mr. ENGEL. Thank you.

Thank you, Mr. Chairman.

Chairman ROYCE. We go now to Mr. Chris Smith from New Jersey.

Mr. SMITH. Thank you very much, Mr. Chairman.

Thank you for your testimony.

A couple of questions. I know this—and I am cognizant this is an open hearing. But do you have reason for optimism that progress is being made in ascertaining the whereabouts of these abducted young women and any indication at all about their welfare and well-being, their health?

Ms. SEWALL. I would say that the team, when I spoke to them yesterday, was very pleased by the level of cooperation, was very pleased by the multiple sources of information flowing into the Intel Fusion Center, was encouraged by the professionalism and the commitment of the Nigerians in the Intel Fusion Center, and was hopeful that the degree of intelligence information would continue to increase over time.

Given time, I am hopeful that we will make progress. And I think that is the extent to which I can respond in this context.

Mr. SMITH. Thank you very much for that.

Let me ask you with regards to the designation of FTO status, which I think is a very serious issue. On July 10, 2012, I chaired a hearing. Assistant Secretary for African Affairs Johnnie Carson testified, and I asked him repeatedly at that time why Boko Haram was not designated a Foreign Terrorist Organization. And he said, while acknowledging it is a very important question, that he believes that the larger element—he goes,

"We believe that the larger element of Boko Haram is not interested in doing anything but attempting to discredit, disgrace the Nigerian Government."

He went on to say—this is Ambassador Carson speaking—

"I would remind people that the phenomena of Boko Haram is one of discrediting the central government in power for its failure to deliver services to the people."

In retrospect, do you believe that was an assessment that had validity, I mean, services to the people, that is why they are doing this?

I would also note parenthetically that Principal Deputy Assistant Secretary Robert Jackson acknowledged last week that, "In retrospect, we might have done the designation earlier." He then added, "I think we will be quicker to make designations based on our own assessments earlier based on this."

I actually went, as you may know, in September of last year to Jos and to Abuja and repeatedly raised the question of Foreign Terrorist Organization designations. And, frankly, in government meetings on the Nigerian side, in meetings with our own people in the Embassy, there was a very strong sense that this could have a very valuable effect, particularly in tracking where all the weapons are coming from.

Maybe they don't have bank accounts. Maybe they do. I don't know. But if we really look and probe and try to discern who is providing the AK–47s and the IEDs and the like that are killing so many people, we may be able to put a tourniquet—or at least begin putting a tourniquet on this bloodshed.

So your sense on that statement that this—you know, statement that was made by, again, Johnnie Carson, "The phenomenon of Boko Haram is one of discrediting the central government in power for its failure to deliver services to the people."

Ms. SEWALL. I think it is hard to look at Boko Haram as an insurgency that rests predominantly on the failings of the State, but there is no question that the failings of the State create a context in which disaffected voices are prey to recruitment.

And when you look at the specifics of Boko Haram's tactics in terms of forcible recruitment of persons, that is a way to explain how it continues to survive, additionally.

I think, from the perspective of our efforts to counter Boko Haram from the outside, from legal mechanisms that exist outside of the Nigerian context in which the Nigerian decisions are central, the important step, to me, was the June 2012 designation of the three leaders as——

Mr. SMITH. Let me just ask you—because I am almost out of time—should we have done the FTO designation earlier?

Ms. SEWALL. I wasn't here; so, I don't know. I think that the most——

Mr. SMITH. You are in a very high position. I look back and forth. We all do all the time.

Ms. SEWALL. Right.

Mr. SMITH. Should it have been done?

Ms. SEWALL. Right. Well, I thank you for your leadership on this important issue. And it is clear that the committee played a very vital role in continuing to press the issue.

I think the important thing is that the three leaders were designated in 2012, and the organization as a whole——

Mr. SMITH. I understand that. I am almost out of time. I will just ask very quickly.

Have there been attacks by Boko Haram against Americans? Jos has the highest number of Americans in Northern Nigeria. Following yesterday's bombings, have all Americans been accounted for? And for the record, when the U.N. compound was bombed, were any Americans present?

Ms. DORY. I am not aware that there were Americans involved in the U.N. compound bombing. And I think, in terms of Jos, we would have to check with the Embassy to see if there is a full accounting of Americans. I am not——

Chairman ROYCE. You can get back to us, then.

Mr. Brad Sherman of California.

Mr. SHERMAN. Thank you.

Ms. Dory, perhaps you could give me a one-word answer. Boko Haram has got a lot of weapons. Are they mostly captured from the Nigerian military, purchased, or we don't know?

Ms. DORY. If I could give slightly more than one word, it is a mixture, in our understanding. They have resources as a result of kidnapping-for-ransom operations. So they are able to purchase, to include——

Mr. SHERMAN. Are the weapons that we have seen them use or captured from their caches or stores the same weapons found in Nigerian military arsenals?

Ms. DORY. Some of them are also captured from Nigerian security services or in raids against arsenals. So it is a mix.

Mr. SHERMAN. Okay.

Dr. Sewall, Mr. Mamman Nur is a high-ranking member of Boko Haram. According to open sources, he may be a key link between that organization and certain AQ affiliates, like Al-Shabaab. He may have been behind the 2011 U.N. bombing.

Should we be designating this individual as a specially designated global terrorist?

Ms. SEWALL. I don't know the answer off the top, and I will have to look into that and get back to you. I simply can't answer that right now. I apologize.

Mr. SHERMAN. There are lots of reports in the press that the Nigerian military knew hours in advance of this attack.

Do either of you have any information that would either confirm or discredit, beyond what we have all read in the newspapers?

Ms. DORY. I am familiar with the press reports, but don't have additional information either way.

Mr. SHERMAN. Dr. Sewall, I am trying to understand the attitude of the Nigerian Government. It is acting as if it is almost disturbed that the whole world is now focused on Boko Haram.

Can you explain why the Nigerian Government wasn't pressing us to designate Boko Haram as a terrorist organization and wasn't doing more to bring in international support in its efforts against this terrorist organization?

Ms. SEWALL. Well, I am not sure I can really speak for the Nigerian Government, but I can share with you, Congressman, my impressions based on the conversations that we had in our recent visit.

And so I think the Nigerian Government believes that it has heard the message about the need to change the way it does its business.

It believes it has taken a more offensive approach in recent months, and it has expressed the belief that the more recent rounds of bombings have been the efforts by a desperate group to gain attention.

I think that the Nigerian view about international attention was misguided in some ways along the same lines that I have heard commentary in the U.S. public discourse, which is to say that the world ignored Nigeria and is now only now focusing on Nigeria with the kidnapping of the schoolgirls.

And so I found myself reiterating the decade-long security cooperation assistance that we had had and the messages that we had been sending them about corruption, about the comportment and accountability——

Mr. SHERMAN. And I will point out we would have designated Boko Haram earlier had we not, I think correctly, taken into consideration the views of the Nigerian Government. It is just, I am confounded as to why the Nigerian Government wasn't pushing us forward, why they were pulling us back.

We have designated certain individuals. We have designated the entire organization. The view I have of Boko Haram is that, of all of the Islamic extremist organizations, they are the ones that are most in the jungle, the least likely to have bank accounts, et cetera.

Have we successfully frozen any of the individual assets of the specially designated global terrorists—frozen any of the assets or been successful in going after Boko Haram?

A lot of discussion here is, "Why didn't we do it sooner?" But we did do it over 6 months ago. And if they are really an in-the-bush organization, that would have very little effect on them, a great effect on us psychologically because we like to feel like we have done something, like we indict Chinese military officers because they are engaged in hacking.

But other than making us feel better, what have we been able to accomplish with all these designations?

Ms. SEWALL. I would need to refer you to my colleagues in other agencies to speak to the specifics of the enforcement actions pursuant to the sanctions designation. And perhaps in the hearing tomorrow——

Mr. SHERMAN. But you are not aware of anything that the designations of certain individuals as specially designated global terrorists or the designation of Boko Haram as a terrorist organization—to your knowledge, there isn't any particular bank account, a particular intercepted or prevented fundraising effort, no tangible effect of 6 months—well, more than 6 months of such designations?

Ms. SEWALL. Unfortunately, I really need to refer you to the colleagues that do the enforcement. I am just not in a position to answer the question. I apologize.

Mr. SHERMAN. I yield back.

Chairman ROYCE. Congressman Sherman, in answer to your first question—or further answer to it—there was testimony from the FBI, and I will just give you their quick response.

FBI Director James Comey testified that Boko Haram has communications, training and weapons links with al-Qaeda in the Maghreb, as well as Al-Shabaab based in Somalia, and al-Qaeda in the Arabian Peninsula based in Yemen.

And then he also testified that these links, in his words, "may strengthen Boko Haram's capacity to conduct terrorist attacks against U.S. or Western targets in the future."

So in terms of the weapons movements, that is the FBI's testimony.

Mr. SHERMAN. It is good to have expertise both from there and from here.

Chairman ROYCE. Right. Right.

We go to Mr. Mike McCaul of Texas.

Mr. MCCAUL. Thank you, Mr. Chairman.

Let me just say, last night I watched the video again of Boko Haram, the leader with these 270 girls, and it is horrific, and it is hard to stand back idly and watch that happen, knowing that we could do more to help them.

The chairman raised the issue of the waiver process. And I guess my question to Dr. Sewall is: If that waiver was granted, what additional assistance could be given to this situation?

Ms. SEWALL. I think one of the distinctions that I have been trying to articulate is that the waiver really is geared toward the training and material support for forces.

And some 50 percent of the Nigerian military at this point in time are not eligible for that form of cooperation with the United States because of the Leahy Law.

So we have been able to engage in security cooperation with Leahy-vetted units, which is the remaining 50 percent.

In terms of the operational pieces, I guess I should turn to my colleague, Ms. Dory, to speak about what additionally might happen in a waiver.

But at this point we are doing everything that the Nigerians want us to be doing, and we are there and available to do more, completely consistent with the Leahy Law, with our deployment teams, and our military planners there in Abuja.

Mr. MCCAUL. Ms. Dory, if that waiver is granted, what additional assistance militarily could be provided?

Ms. DORY. Sir, it is predominantly a function of what type of assistance is requested by the Government of Nigeria. We have a complete menu of training activities, equipping activities, advising, assisting, the usual inventory that the Department can pursue in partnership with another country. But it really rests with the host nation to identify in what areas it wishes to cooperate.

Mr. MCCAUL. You mentioned earlier that a military operation would be risky and risky to the hostages, and I understand that.

But has there been any effort to have our FBI's hostage rescue team assist with this?

Ms. DORY. There are FBI personnel who are part of the multidisciplinary team, and I believe the services of the FBI's hostage recovery experts are on the table.

Mr. MCCAUL. Well, I would hope so. I would hope the answer is ''yes'' to that question. I think they could be very valuable in this situation.

I chair the Homeland Security Committee. In 2011, we released a report, ''Intel: Boko Haram Emerging Threat to the Homeland.''

We asked that they be designated as an FTO back then because it would support U.S. intelligence in their effort to curb financing, to isolate it internationally, heighten public awareness, and signal to other governments that the threat is serious.

In September 2013, we issued a follow-up report, ''Boko Haram, the Growing Threat to the Homeland,'' again asking that the designation take place. Members of Congress additionally made that request.

And, finally, the head of the Justice Department's National Security Division sent a letter to the State Department requesting that Boko Haram be put on this list.

Now, I know, Dr. Sewall, that, eventually, they were put on the list. But, you know, it took years to get the Haqqani Network put on the list. It took years to get Ansar al-Sharia behind the Benghazi attack put on this list. We still can't get the Quds Force to be put on this list.

Why is it so difficult for the State Department to put what is so obvious on the Foreign Terrorist Organization list?

Ms. SEWALL. I can't speak to the decisions that were made before I came to the Department, sir. I am sorry.

And I know that there are many different considerations that go into other decisions. I mean, in the context of the Nigerian case, I think I explained that there was a discussion with the government, there was a discussion about the nature of the threat, and there was a discussion about the efficacy, the true impact of the sanctions.

I can only speak to that case, and I unfortunately can't speak to the prior cases.

Mr. McCAUL. Well, it is not just Members of Congress. It is not just the Justice Department. It is General Hamm. Carter Hamm talked about this threat. Director Clapper, the DNI, mentioned this threat. General Dave Rodriguez, Commander of AFRICOM.

This is coming in from multiple points, you know, not just Members of Congress, not my committee, but multiple points in the military, the Justice Department.

I don't really understand, when you look at that video, when it is so obvious that they are terrorists, why they weren't put on the FTO, which just maybe—it may not have stopped this event from happening, but at least we could have put some pressure on their financial ties and their funding mechanisms.

With that, Mr. Chairman, I yield back.

Chairman ROYCE. We go now to Mr. Gregory Meeks from New York.

Mr. MEEKS. Thank you, Mr. Chairman.

First, Mr. Chairman, I want to thank you for the way that you have been conducting this hearing and the investigations and the education that you have done to talk about the waiver, to figure out how we resolve this.

You have done it in a manner—and I think I want the record to be clear with me that I concur with you and your opinion on how we should be able to assist the Nigerian Government.

I think that the research that you and your staff have done is excellent, and I want the record to reflect that this is clearly something that we all agree upon in that regard.

I want to say to Ms. Peter, who is sitting in the audience, who I had to listen to her tell the horrible story in regards to her family that happened before her eyes in 2011. No child, no child, should have to see their parents killed and siblings before their eyes. None. And it really angers me inside when I hear that.

And when you hear and see this group, Boko Haram, who now has kidnapped these 200 girls, but has killed boys, destroyed churches, taken away hope, there is no redeeming factor for individuals like that.

They are in the same category as al-Qaeda and Al-Shabaab, and I want to make sure that we do everything that we can to free those girls. I don't care whether it is negotiation, whatever it is.

But let me tell you I don't want that to be the end of it. You know, generally, I am a multilateral guy. And I think all of the countries—I haven't heard any country, anybody, dissent on the evil of this group.

So I want somebody—I don't see why that, once we get these girls free—I am going to tell you, for me, I want drones, I want something, because they don't belong on this earth.

Threatening people and having people living in fear, this is something that I see that this world—not just this Nation, but other nations all across, are coming together to say, "We are going to stop this."

And we need to do it. We need to do it in Nigeria. We need to do it in Syria, Pakistan and Somalia, wherever Al-Shabaab—wherever these individuals are.

And then we have got to do more than that, because the attacks on these girls—over 200 schoolgirls in Northern Nigeria—we talked about it and it is a global outcry to keep children safe in schools and protect their right to education. But, unfortunately, we are all too aware of these same groups—extremist groups that are doing the same thing.

So I am wondering whether or not there is a plan to ensure that children—all children, especially those in conflicted areas, are protected and have access to quality education.

I know you can't answer that question, but I am just upset right now. I wish I could think rationally, as the chairman does and has done.

That is why I think that it is a good thing that he is doing this because you need rational thinkers at a time like this and not having emotions taking over, as it is doing with me.

But I am. Just listening to Ms. Peter's story has made me that I can't, you know, do what the chairman has done. So I thank God that the chairman is doing what he is doing right now.

But, you know, it seems to me that I have got, like Ms. Peter, the same year—15-, 14-year-old daughter, who is asking me about this scenario and what are we doing and what should we do. So when I am thinking that, I can't think rationally.

Tell me why—Ms. Sewall?

Ms. SEWALL. First, Congressman Meeks, I want to tell you that I can be every bit as irrational as you are on this issue. I don't think there is a single American that doesn't detest Boko Haram from the bottom of their hearts.

I have four daughters. I have three 17-year-old daughters and I have one 12-year-old daughter. And when I left them to go to Nigeria, you can imagine how heavily they weighed on my heart.

And when I met with the activists that had been protesting the government's response to the crisis, when I called the principal of the school to express Americans' support for her and for bringing the girls back safely, I was able to give voice to the emotion that I think we all feel in the context of this immediate crisis.

At the same time, it is abundantly clear that, if we are to move to address Boko Haram as an enduring threat beyond the question of these 200-plus schoolgirls, that the Nigerian Government itself has to make changes. It has to address corruption. It has to address the excessive use of violence.

There are ways we can support them in those efforts, and there are ways that we can do specific things for them. But those are fleeting things. Those will not solve the Boko Haram problem.

The Boko Haram problem in Nigeria needs to be addressed by Nigerians. The Boko Haram problem, as a regional threat, needs to be addressed by the regional actors.

The value of this crisis is that it has brought together in a conversation all the actors that are seized not just with the schoolgirls, but with the enduring threat of Boko Haram.

And this moment offers the hope that we will coordinate the assistance and focus the efforts to address the underlying problems here, which are the scourge of Boko Haram. But any sustained solution requires the Government of Nigeria to show a degree of commitment and to take a set of actions that it has thus far not committed to.

And so we cannot lose sight of the fact that this is not our problem to solve, and we must seize the moment to bring together all of the voices of concern about the schoolgirls and about Boko Haram to press and support the Nigerian Government in undertaking its own critical changes and reforms.

Chairman ROYCE. Thank you, Mr. Meeks.

We go now to Mr. Jeff Duncan of South Carolina.

Mr. DUNCAN. Well, thank you, Mr. Chairman.

And I want to thank Mr. Meeks for his passion on this issue. It is touching. And I share your passion.

I just hope that that same passion will continue to carry forward as we talk about terrorists wherever they are, whoever they are, attacking not just interests in Africa, but Americans and folks that love liberty anywhere in the world. And so I appreciate that and look forward to working with you going forward.

I listened to Ms. Peter's story. And thinking about Christians, in general, her father was a pastor. Her brother could have grown up to be a pastor, is what the terrorists thought.

So the question I have for you, Ms. Sewall: Do you think Christians are specifically targeted in the Boko Haram attacks?

Ms. SEWALL. I wish there was such discrimination in Boko Haram attacks. Boko Haram attacks everyone who is Nigerian. Boko Haram is an equal-opportunity threat for all Nigerian citizens.

Mr. DUNCAN. Thank you for that.

I would like to delve into the links with al-Qaeda and the broader al-Qaeda network.

Boko Haram's ties to other al-Qaeda-affiliated and associated groups, as well as the focus by some of its members on pursuing a more transnational agenda, have amplified concerns of the group's threat.

U.S. officials have suggested that Boko Haram and al-Qaeda in the Islamic Maghreb, or the AQIM, were likely sharing funds, training, and explosive materials.

So could you provide some clarity—and I am going to ask both of you this question and ask you to be brief—but could you provide some clarity to the extent of cooperation and support that AQIM has provided to this organization.

Ms. DORY. Congressman——

Mr. DUNCAN. Financial, material support. All that, please.

Ms. DORY. In this setting, there are limits on the ability to go into detail. But we can absolutely confirm the categories that you are talking about in terms of the cooperation between Boko Haram and AQIM, in particular, where the ties seem to be the strongest, that it does include training, facilitation, financing of weapons. That is the type of influence and material that is being traded back and forth between AQIM and Boko Haram.

Boko Haram also has sought linkages with some of the other AQ affiliates, as was discussed earlier, and the intensity of those linkages is less clear.

But there is an all-member briefing tomorrow, at which I think—a classified briefing tomorrow where we could get into some of those details.

Mr. DUNCAN. Ms. Sewall, a question that just came to mind: What is the State Department, the FBI, Treasury, doing to track the money?

Do we have folks on the ground working with the financial institutions in and around Nigeria and Africa, in general, to trace this money to make sure that we know the sources and whether there are any al-Qaeda links?

Can you tell me what we are doing in that regard, if anything?

Ms. SEWALL. Congressman, I wish I could. I don't have the details on that. But I would be happy to go back to the other agencies and to the specific elements of the State Department that might be involved in this and get you a more fulsome answer.

Mr. DUNCAN. Okay. I appreciate that.

The other thing is: Can you answer the question about the extent of the cooperation that you know of between Boko Haram and al-Qaeda affiliates? Material support, financial, anything you might be able to add.

Ms. SEWALL. Our understanding is that there is intermittent support as much as Deputy Assistant Secretary of Defense Dory described.

Mr. DUNCAN. Are we connecting those dots within the State Department?

Ms. SEWALL. Sir, the State Department is always working hard to connect the dots.

Mr. DUNCAN. Have any of the Nigerians who have been prosecuted in U.S. courts in recent years for providing material support to terrorist groups such as AQAP had any links to the Boko Haram group? Do you know of any connections?

Ms. SEWALL. I don't. But, again, I am not fully briefed to answer that question to 100 percent certainty. And so I would have to take it for the record, also.

Mr. DUNCAN. Okay. Last question before my time runs out: Have we identified individuals within Boko Haram and put them on the terrorist watch list to make sure that they don't infiltrate the United States of America?

Do we know who these leaders are, members of this terrorist organization? Have we put them on the list to make sure they are not going to infiltrate the United States of America?

Ms. SEWALL. I would be surprised if we haven't, given that they have been designated as specially designated terrorists themselves. But that is a DHS function. And so I can check on that and get back to you as well.

Mr. DUNCAN. Thank you so much.

Mr. Chairman, I yield back.

Chairman ROYCE. Thank you.

We go now to Mr. David Cicilline of Rhode Island.

Mr. CICILLINE. Thank you, Mr. Chairman. Thank you for this hearing, and thank you for your sensitivity in bringing Deborah Peter to us for our conversation earlier before this hearing.

It has been a tremendous honor to meet with her and to see her extraordinary courage and horrifying to hear the story of how she and her family were so brutalized by Boko Haram.

I know that every member of this committee is committed to doing everything we can to hold these individuals accountable and to rescue these girls.

So thank you for being with us today, Deborah.

When you look at the information we have learned about the impact of this terrorist organization, in addition to more than 4,000 people having been killed in Boko Haram-related violence, U.N. and Nigerian officials report that more than 6 million Nigerians have been affected and more than 300,000 Nigerians have been displaced.

So I think it is really important for us to understand and for the world to understand the significant impact of this terrorist organization.

So my first question to either Dr. Sewall or Ms. Dory is: Do we have a sense of where Boko Haram gets its resources, its weaponry and its financial support?

Ms. DORY. Congressman, I think I have briefly touched on this already. But it is a variety of sources in terms of their access to finances and equipment.

Some of it comes from their activities in Nigeria, whether it is stealing resources, food, equipment from local populations, whether it is taking them from the military and other security services in the course of attacks.

You may be familiar with an incident where they destroyed aircraft at a Nigerian Air Force base, for example. So that is one source.

They also, through kidnapping for ransom schemes, have financial resources at their disposal. So they are able to purchase weapons and supplies on the open market, and there is a connection into the Libyan arms markets in that regard.

Mr. CICILLINE. And I know that you have said, Ms. Dory, that the principal responsibility for defeating Boko Haram has to come from the Nigerian people and that requires them to focus on governance issues, reductions of corruption, ending mass arrests and disappearances within the government, and their own human rights record.

So what can we do and—what is the U.S. doing or what can we do in addition to that to pressure the Nigerians to do that so they have the capacity to respond to Boko Haram?

And what kind of leverage do we really have in this moment to really make that case with the Nigerian Government? And do you see any signs that they are serious about undertaking whatever those recommendations might be?

Ms. DORY. I will take the question and, also, share it with my colleague.

I think the head-of-state-to-head-of-state engagement that we have seen over this issue is indicative of both our level of concern and our level of support and our willingness to communicate it at the highest levels.

So I think this is a very important time, both in terms of the U.S. support and determination and, coupled with that, from colleagues from around the world, all over Europe and beyond, who are similarly outraged at the situation and resolved that now is the time to provide maximum support and pressure as we engage with the Government of Nigeria.

Mr. CICILLINE. Last issue I just want to mention.

I have been working on a piece of legislation to address this situation in which there is an emergency necessitating—or that should authorize the issuance of a visa. And I am just curious.

It seems as if—this related, actually, to a mother who was attempting to come back to the United States to retrieve a child who had been murdered in the U.S. for burial back in their home country.

And there was actually not a provision in the existing State Department protocol because she had no—not deep ties in her home country, no business, no employment.

So, obviously, they argued that there was not a sufficient basis to give her a visa for fear she would overstay it and remain here.

But in the example that we heard about this morning, it seems as if I am on the right track in trying to develop some exemption, some emergency issuance of a visa, for those who have been victims of terrorism or—you know, we can set out the criteria.

But it sounded, at least initially, that Deborah was in a situation in which she was not given a visa, which I think everyone agrees doesn't make sense. And I would just like your thoughts on that.

Ms. SEWALL. I am sorry. I really know very little about the visa process. And so I just don't feel comfortable commenting. Thank you.

Mr. CICILLINE. Thank you.

I yield back, Mr. Chairman.

Chairman ROYCE. Thank you.

We go to Mr. Mo Brooks of Alabama.

Mr. BROOKS. Thank you, Mr. Chairman.

In your judgment, does Nigeria currently have the police or military capability of defeating Boko Haram?

Ms. DORY. Congressman, from my perspective, Nigeria's military is the force with which I am most familiar. And they have been a premier peacekeeping force for many decades, focused external to their country, if you think about their long history in that regard.

And the process of retooling from a peacekeeping orientation to focusing on a domestic insurgency is something that takes an entire recalibration in terms of how you engage in your home country.

I would say——

Mr. BROOKS. Might I infer from your comments that you just made that the answer is "no," that, as of today, they don't, that things have to be done before they have that capability?

Ms. DORY. Part of it. When we speak of a capability, part of it is the strategic approach and the mindset. And, as yet, Nigeria has not yet finalized a counterterrorism strategic approach. Which, I think, leaves gaps in terms of the operational employment of the security forces, their training and readiness for those types of missions and then the equipment that is available to them.

Mr. BROOKS. Dr. Sewall, do you have a judgment on whether the Nigerian police or military have the capability of defeating Boko Haram as of today?

Ms. SEWALL. It is a great question, and I want to answer it thoroughly. So I have to step back for just one moment and say that the ability of a police force or a military force to effectively defeat a virulent insurgency is limited.

And so that is just the first point to make, that this is why the U.S. has been in a dialogue with the Nigerians for the need for a holistic approach that includes economic development, social engagement, political empowerment and a host of other things.

In a narrow sense, the Nigerians have capability that we would recognize as strong in the sense that they have a number of forces, they have a certain number of equipment.

I think the challenge for both the police and the military is how their assets and resources, human and otherwise, are actually deployed.

And that is why the questions about corruption and that is why the questions about, as DEPSEC Dory just said, the mindset are so critical.

It took us——

Mr. BROOKS. I am not sure if I am getting a response. I am trying to get something simple, a "yes," "no" or "I don't know."

Do you have a judgment as to whether the Nigerian police and military have the capability as of today to defeat Boko Haram? "Yes," "no" or "I don't know."

Ms. SEWALL. So the United States, when it began its invasion in Iraq, was the finest military force in the world——

Mr. BROOKS. I am sorry.

Ms. SEWALL [continuing]. And it was unable to——

Mr. BROOKS. I am asking for a "yes," "no" or "I don't know" because I have limited time here. I can't go into a monologue.

Ms. SEWALL. It is complicated.

Mr. BROOKS. It is complicated.

So maybe, maybe not? Is that a fair way to assess your opinion.

Ms. SEWALL. If you wish to describe it that way, that——

Mr. BROOKS. Well, what short answer can you give me that describes your opinion of whether Boko Haram today can be defeated by the Nigerian police and/or military?

Ms. SEWALL. I think that, with the appropriate political redirection, as well as the concerted effort on the part of specific capabilities, that the country of Nigeria, the Government of Nigeria, can make significant progress in defeating Boko Haram.

Completely eliminating, I would hedge on that. The timeframe, I would hedge on that. But I don't think there is any question that the Government of Nigeria both can and will——

Mr. BROOKS. Thank you for your response.

The very first sentence of the Charter of the United States in Chapter I, Article I, Paragraph 1, states:

"The Purposes of the United Nations are: To maintain international peace and security, and to that end: To take effective collective measures for the prevention of threats to the peace, and for the suppression of acts of aggression or other breaches of the peace.''

If we were to look at the history of Boko Haram in Nigeria: August 26, 2011, a bomb attack on a U.N. building, 21 killed; January 20, 2012, attacks in Kano State, 12 targets, over 150 people killed.

We have already talked about the young schoolgirls who were kidnapped. May 5, 2014, an attack lasting 12 hours, 300 people killed. The list goes on and on and on. You have provided two pages of attacks.

As of today, what has the Obama administration undertaken to secure a United Nations force to take on Boko Haram inasmuch as that seems to be the primary purpose of the United Nations Charter?

Ms. SEWALL. So, the United Nations Charter, as you know, is based on the concept of sovereignty. And so, typically, when there is an insurgency within a government, the government is expected to address the security threat and is free to seek assistance.

Terrorism has typically been treated in a slightly different venue. Boko Haram has elements of both. And so I think that it is certainly—that there are a variety of ways in which the international community can respond to what is increasingly recognized as——

Mr. BROOKS. Okay. Again, I don't think you are responding to my question.

My question was: What has the Obama administration done to request the kind of support from the United Nations that we would need to eliminate Boko Haram's influence in Nigeria and Central Africa inasmuch as that is the primary purpose of the United Nations?

I don't know how we can be any clearer when the United Nations says in its Charter:

''[T]o take effective collective measures for the prevention [and removal] of threats to the peace, and for the suppression of acts of aggression . . .''

So what has the Obama administration done to invoke the United Nation's charter to get the United Nations to do their job?

Ms. SEWALL. Right now, the way the Obama administration has interacted with the United Nations on the question of Boko Haram is to encourage the Nigerian Government to designate Boko Haram pursuant to the al-Qaeda list.

What the United States and the Obama administration has been doing since President Obama has been in power is working to strengthen Nigeria's capacity to defeat Boko Haram. So we have been very actively engaged in this. This engagement began before the Obama administration.

And, ultimately, the Nigerian Government has great progress that it can make to defeat Boko Haram. It needs to decide and commit itself to do that in ways that are similar to those learning curves that we, the United States, have had to take in defeat- ing—

——

Mr. BROOKS. Thank you, Mr. Chairman, for indulging.

Chairman ROYCE. Thank you.

We go to Gerry Connolly of Virginia.

Mr. CONNOLLY. Thank you, Mr. Chairman.

Here we go again. So, Dr. Sewall, clearly it is the fault of the Obama administration that these young girls were kidnapped. Is that true?

Ms. SEWALL. No.

Mr. CONNOLLY. Someone in the administration embedded with Boko Haram?

Ms. SEWALL. Do you really want me to answer the question?

Mr. CONNOLLY. Yes, ma'am.

Ms. SEWALL. No, sir.

Mr. CONNOLLY. No.

Conspiracy to turn a blind eye to the activities of Boko Haram?

Ms. SEWALL. No, sir.

Mr. CONNOLLY. Changing talking points to make sure that somehow the administration was protected even at the expense of innocent victims of Boko Haram?

Ms. SEWALL. No, sir.

Mr. CONNOLLY. Dilatory tactics by the administration to prevent effective action by the United Nations, well known, I might say to my friend from Alabama, for its effective actions.

So we were engaged in some kind of activity in New York to slow it down and not designate them in a timely fashion or coordinate international reaction to the unspeakable outrage of the kidnapping of these young women?

Ms. SEWALL. I would argue that the United States has been among the most concerned about Boko Haram for the longest period of time among all the actors within the international community.

Mr. CONNOLLY. Including at the United Nations?

Ms. SEWALL. It has been a concern of American officials for some time, as evidenced by our significant both personnel and financial investments in enhancing——

Mr. CONNOLLY. Including at the United Nations?

Ms. SEWALL. Including at the United Nations insofar as we have been supporting Nigeria's efforts to designate the terrorist organization.

Mr. CONNOLLY. Thank you.

So, I guess, from your testimony, there is no evidence whatsoever of anything other than an administration deeply concerned and doing everything in its power to try to assist the international community and the Government of Nigeria and, when necessary, to prod the Government of Nigeria to try to take effective action to defang Boko Haram and to release these young women. Is that correct?

Ms. SEWALL. It is a high priority of the United States Government, and we have been consistent in our efforts. Yes.

Mr. CONNOLLY. It just strikes me as something not worthy of the Congress, when we actually continue to fall into a false narrative, to try to make partisan political points when we are trying to do foreign policy.

There used to be a time—it was actually a Republican who pronounced the philosophy that our partisan differences ended at the water's edge for the sake of the country.

And it just seems to me something deplorable that any of us would yield to the temptation—no one here, of course—to try to make political points off of this kind of tragedy and to hold the President and his administration somehow responsible for every event, especially every unsavory or tragic event, that occurs around the world is simply nonsensical. It may play well on certain networks with certain pundits, but it is not worthy of a great country and it is not worthy of this Congress.

Why can't we come together to try to support a cohesive policy to effectuate the goal, which is to lessen and dismantle Boko Haram and to release safely these young women to their families and try to prevent that kind of kidnapping activity from ever recurring again? Isn't that really the goal of the United States Government, Dr. Sewall? Ms. Dory?

And I need you to answer on the record. A shaking head doesn't—we can't record that.

Ms. SEWALL. I think all Americans share a concern about the schoolgirls and the threat from Boko Haram, and I believe that the United States will be stronger in supporting the desires of the American people, as it speaks with one voice, in that regard.

Mr. CONNOLLY. Ms. Dory?

Ms. DORY. I agree with the objectives as you laid out, the safe recovery of the schoolgirls and the effective addressing of Boko Haram as a threat to Nigeria and the broader region.

Mr. CONNOLLY. And those are our goals? Those are the goals of this government. Is that correct?

Ms. DORY. Those are among our many goals when we are relating to Nigeria and in the broader region.

Mr. CONNOLLY. Yes. I am talking specifically, since this hearing is focused on that, about the Boko Haram activity.

And, obviously, it is not only the desire of all Americans, Dr. Sewall. It is, in fact, the pronounced policy of the United States Government that we want them released. Is that not correct?

Ms. SEWALL. That is correct. General Rodriguez and I traveled to Nigeria to convey that very point.

Mr. CONNOLLY. That is right.

And one final question: Can you both reassure us that our Government is doing everything in its power to effectuate that end?

Ms. SEWALL. The President, the Secretary of State, and the entire government is doing everything it can to effectuate that end.

Mr. CONNOLLY. And from the Defense Department point of view, Ms. Dory?

Ms. DORY. We have brought our maximum effort into the engagement with the Nigerians and hope we can support them in whatever way they will let us.

Mr. CONNOLLY. I thank you both for your testimony. And I assure you there are many of us up here who will be behind you and side by side in trying to make that happen.

Thank you for your service to your country, and thank you for trying to help us achieve a positive end in this tragic set of events.

Thank you, Mr. Chairman.

Chairman ROYCE. Mr. Scott Perry of Pennsylvania.

Mr. PERRY. Thank you, Mr. Chairman.

Dr. Sewall, it is my understanding that officials have repeated—administration officials have repeatedly stated that Boko Haram is not motivated by religious causes, but by issues of economic deprivation.

Is the State Department also led to that conclusion?

Ms. SEWALL. I am not sure whether there is a piece of paper that describes the State Department's view about the motivations of Boko Haram.

What I can tell you is that we know from watching Boko Haram over the years that they are bent on destroying institutions that support the people of Nigeria in the northeast and that they have no compunction about killing any Nigerian that is in their path.

Mr. PERRY. I understand that. And I think we, as Americans, understand that.

But I am trying to focus on how State Department views Boko Haram and——

Ms. SEWALL. We view Boko Haram as a terrorist organization.

Mr. PERRY. Okay. And what is their motivation? If you could, describe that. What are they motivated by? Not what are their actions. What are they motivated by?

Ms. SEWALL. Well, I am not in the head of their leader. I have watched the video like you have. And so I——

Mr. PERRY. I understand.

But you make assessments. You must make assessments.

Ms. SEWALL. We do make assessments.

Mr. PERRY. To understand the adversary and the enemy, you must make assessments.

Ms. SEWALL. We do make assessments. As in the case of the LRA, sometimes it is easier to discern motivations than others.

Al-Qaeda is very clear about its motivations. Some other terrorist organizations are a combination of criminally motivated, egomaniacally motivated, and opportunistic.

And so I just——

Mr. PERRY. Would you accept that they are motivated by religious fanaticism—extremist Islamic religious fanaticism?

Ms. SEWALL. I can speak to the elements of religion that——

Mr. PERRY. I know you can speak to it.

Is that a clear assessment or would you assess it somehow differently than I have just stated?

Ms. SEWALL. If you are asking for an official State Department assessment of the motivations of the leader of Boko Haram, I will need to take that question back and return it to you later.

Mr. PERRY. All right. Well, I just want to give you this information and you can roll that up into your assessment.

The leader of Boko Haram says that, ''Nobody can stop us and live in peace except if you accept Islam and live by sharia law.''

He also said that they will kill anyone who stands against the will of Allah by opposing sharia and that they are fighting a religious war against the Christians and has also said, ''By Allah, we will kill whoever practices democracy.''

When he says things like that and he says that nobody can live in peace except if you accept Islam and live by sharia, do you see any economic nexus there?

Ms. SEWALL. When he talks about religion as one lens through which he defines his enemies, I think that is very revealing. When he talks about democracy as being one lens through which he defines his enemies, I think that is very revealing.

When he decides that killing people who are seeking an education, it constitutes his ideology. I think that is very revealing.

So I think it is a mix of things, among which clearly, in his rhetoric, religion is very important.

Mr. PERRY. Well, is there an economic—because I have heard the administration—I have got reports of the administration saying——

Ms. SEWALL. Okay, I understand now. Yes.

So the economic nexus is something that we have learned through our own experience with combating both violent extremism and counterinsurgency, which is to say, if you have a well-governed, economically vibrant society, you are less likely to have disenfranchised persons who can be lured by extremist ideology of any type.

Mr. PERRY. I understand the lure.

But that has nothing to do with their motivation. That is how they recruit. Their motivation is otherwise. And I am concerned about——

Ms. SEWALL. Their motivation is economic insofar as DEPSEC Dory was talking about kidnap for ransom as being a means of financing themselves.

Mr. PERRY. I understand that is the way of financing.

But administration officials say that their motivation, the reason they exist, is due to economic deprivation that they don't have.

But there are many countries and many people around the world that don't have and that don't resort to kidnappings, killings, bombings, and forced views on extremist religious ideology. But I move on.

Does the administration—does the State Department accept and acknowledge that there is a nexus with Boko Haram and at least its leadership and the Muslim Brotherhood?

Ms. SEWALL. Do you want to speak to that? I don't know.

Mr. PERRY. Quickly, please, if you could.

Ms. DORY. Congressman, from the Department of Defense perspective, I am not aware of a linkage. But I would be glad to take that back.

Mr. PERRY. All right. Well, I have got the linkage here which shows where the leaders came from—and it goes way back to the 1980s—the Muslim Brotherhood.

And here is my concern in my last 15 seconds. It seems to me in some ways that the State Department is living in some altered state of reality, that most of America, yet most of the world, understands and recognizes and, if you can't acknowledge your adversary and your enemy for who they are, there is going to be no way that you can combat them effectively.

And I appreciate, Mr. Chairman, just your indulgence as I close up.

This holistic approach should include something in the national security strategy. And I can see no inclusion in the national security strategy that either of you folks are following. And that is my concern, because we can't fix the problem if we don't identify it.

Thank you, Mr. Chairman.

Chairman ROYCE. Mr. Juan Vargas of California.

Mr. VARGAS. Mr. Chairman, thank you very much for the opportunity to speak.

I have to say I think you can see the emotions up here, because we are very much outraged with what has happened, and I think the American people are outraged.

But I have to ask this question: Where is the Muslim outrage? I mean, I have to say that, if this happened and they did it in the name of Christ, from the Pope on down to the street preacher, everyone would be yelling and screaming, "This is not right. This does not follow our religion. It is wrong" and people would try to find these girls and these people.

So, I mean, I ask: Where is the outrage from the imams? Where is the outrage? This is an insult to Islam. It has to be. They are a peaceful people.

I had the opportunity and the privilege of having a Muslim family live with me and my family for 2 years because of what was going on in Kosovo. So we adopted this family and they lived with us.

And they are wonderful people and they lived peacefully. And they have two girls. I have two girls. And I have to say I love my daughters as much as they love their daughters.

I have to ask: Where is the outrage? Could you answer?

I mean, again, if this was happening in the name of Christianity, every official Christian group from, you know, the Catholics down to the unorganized Christians, everyone would think this was the biggest scandal in the world.

Where is the outrage?

Ms. SEWALL. Well, where I heard the outrage when I was in Abuja was from the voices that were demonstrating in the public squares, which included community leaders and just community members and concerned citizens, many of them from the Borno State, who were by and large Muslim, and were outraged at the perversion of Islamic tenets in the rhetoric of the Boko Haram leadership.

So I think certainly in the context of Nigeria there is outrage and it comes from the community that is most affected by these events.

Mr. VARGAS. Well, I have to say it doesn't seem like it. I mean, as someone who watches the news all the time and I know that the Muslim community in the world has gotten outraged over other things, where they protested in the street and, you know, have gotten very angry, understandably so in some instances, I don't see that here.

I mean, I see us fighting and very frustrated over this issue. I see us, you know, fighting over whether the administration is doing enough, "Why aren't we sending the soldiers?," you know, "We have people there. We ought to go out and find them and shoot them and kill them and rescue these girls."

I mean, that is basically what we are saying up here. And we are frustrated because we don't seem to be able to do that. It violates a lot of laws. But I think, as every parent, that is what we want to do, go find the bad guys and put them away or shoot them.

But you don't see—you don't feel this outrage in the rest of the Muslim world. You don't see it. It is shocking to me. You would think that they would be turning in these people and saying, "Here they are. Come and get them. Here they are."

And you don't seem to—maybe you could tell us. Maybe you will tell us in a secured situation, a classified briefing.

But is there that type of help in the community there? Are they helping us find the bad guys?

Ms. SEWALL. So if the question is whether tactically on the ground there is an outpouring of support to identify the Boko Haram people, I think the way to characterize the situation in Nigeria is that Boko Haram has so terrorized the local population that they are very fearful of being perceived as participants in the war by actively cooperating with the government.

The situation, of course, is greatly complicated by the fact that security forces from the 7th Division have often, in their pursuit of Boko Haram, killed numerous civilians in addition to Boko Haram. So by virtue of trying to draw attention to an area, they could be jeopardizing their own children. And so it is very difficult——

Mr. VARGAS. No. That part is understandable.

I mean, you know, no one is saying that the Nigerian Government has clean hands here. I mean, I think that is the issue.

They have done some terrible things, and that is why I think the population has a lot of issues. I mean, that is the underlying problem you are trying to solve.

But at the same time, it seems, if there was more outrage in the Muslim world, there would be more pressure to try to find these guys and rescue these girls, and there doesn't seem to be.

I guess that is really my question.

And I will yield back after that, Mr. Chairman.

But, again, I find it disturbing that there is not more outrage, that the outrage comes from the Western world and the outrage should be coming from the Muslim world. We have got to do something here.

Thank you.

Chairman ROYCE. Thank you, Mr. Vargas.

Ms. Dory has to be at the Pentagon for a meeting at noon, and we appreciate her being here this morning.

I will remind members of an all-House closed session on Boko Haram, which Eliot Engel and I and the House will be doing tomorrow.

Dr. Sewall has agreed to finish with our members who remain. So we appreciate that very much.

But, Ms. Dory, we will let you go. Thank you.

We go now to Ron DeSantis from Florida. Mr.

DeSANTIS. Thank you, Mr. Chairman.

Dr. Sewall, I have been a little concerned with what I have heard in two of the colloquies. I know that my colleague from South Carolina, Mr. Duncan, had asked whether the Boko Haram attack on the schoolgirls was anti-Christian in nature, whether that was one of their motivations, and you seemed to suggest that it was not.

Did I hear you correctly?

52

Ms. SEWALL. I believe what you heard me say is that the attack was against Nigerian schoolgirls.

Mr. DeSantis. But you don't think that it was an attack motivated by being anti-Christian at all?

Ms. SEWALL. Again, you are asking for—speaking to motivation when I am unable to be in the mind of someone and, I hope, never to be in the mind of someone like the leader of Boko Haram.

Mr. DeSantis. And I don't expect you to. But I do think that——

Ms. SEWALL. And, of course, in the case of the schoolgirls, I believe it was some 15 percent of them were Muslim. So it was the education and the freedom and empowerment and the progress that Boko Haram was attacking as it attacked the schoolgirls, as much as it was anything to do with religion.

I am not denying that religion doesn't appear to be a very important factor for the leadership, but that is—that is different from saying it is the sole motivation. It is different from trying to understand the impact of their actions on Muslim civilians throughout the northeast.

Mr. DeSantis. And I appreciate that. And certainly you can't get into their head. I just—and I don't necessarily say that it is the sole motivation, but I think we have to realize that this is an animating feature.

I mean, you can't get into his head, but you can listen to what he says. And he said—and this is quoting from his speech—''We know what is happening in the world. It is a Jihad war against Christians and Christianity. It is a war against Western education, democracy, and constitution. This is a war against Christians and democracy. In their constitution, Allah says we should finish them when we get them.''

So, clearly he believes that Christianity, constitutionalism, liberal democracy—he is putting those things together and he is saying that his belief and his version of Islam is what is motivating him to do that.

And I think to try to—I mean, there was a colloquy with Mr. Perry about—you know, are they an Islamic terrorist group? Would you feel confident putting the fact that, yeah, there are terrorist groups specifically operating in the name of Islam?

Ms. SEWALL. Well, again, you know, when they recruit people forcibly and make them fight for them, I don't know what percentage of their force is essentially enslaved and what percentage of their force represents the extreme and neolithic views of the leadership.

I agree with you completely that their rhetoric includes significant religious motivation, but it also includes motivation that reflects westernization more broadly.

We know that modernization and westernization and education, for that matter, is an equal-opportunity, inclusive of all faiths process. And so they are motivated by something that goes beyond just Christianity based on what they say and what they do.

Mr. DeSantis. But the modernity conflicts with their faith, and that is—and when he started his speech, he said, ''My brethren in Islam, I am greeting you in the name of Allah, like he instructed we should among Muslims. Allah is great and has given us the privilege and temerity above all people.'' So the anti-Western posture is flowing from this belief.

And it is interesting. You read his speech, you know, and he starts getting into all kinds of issues. He says that he believes in marrying off 9-year-old girls. He thinks that is acceptable, and he cited a religious justification, the conduct of Muhammad, for that. He defends slavery and criticizes human rights. Again, he cited Islam as the reason for that. He threatens to kill the President of the United States.

And so I think what we are dealing with here is—I mean, you see the video of those schoolgirls being forced to wear Islamic garb, being forced to recite the Koran. He is trying to spread this ideology.

This group is spreading the ideology by the sword because they know that it is fundamentally at odds with human reason and that, if these girls are allowed to be educated in that school, they are obviously not going to think that his ideology is something that is very attractive.

So that is what we are dealing with here, and I just hope that we can understand the motivation. If we try to put a Western frame of reference on how they behave and say, Well, maybe it is because they think there is some economic problems or this or that, you know, some of those things may be a factor at the margins.

But at the end of the day, I think that that speech and their conduct make clear what their motivation is. And so I would just hope that we would be willing and always have our eyes open and not try to blind ourselves to reality.

And I yield back.

Chairman ROYCE. We go now to Lois Frankel from Florida.

Ms. FRANKEL. Thank you, Mr. Chair.

Thank you, Dr. Sewall, for being a very calm-sounding board here today and, Mr. Chair, for this bipartisanship. I would call it a bipartisan show of humanity.

And I very much enjoyed meeting today also with Deborah Peter, who has a lovely sparkle in her eye and a lovely smile, wonderful resilience.

And she told us a very sad story of how she basically fled Nigeria 2 years ago after she witnessed the murder of her father and her brother and—because her father was the pastor of a Christian church.

And then her 14-year-old brother was shot because, as Deborah related, her—one of the terrorists said, ''Well, he will grow up to be the pastor of the church.''

I hope, Mr. Chair, that we are going to be able to help her with her visa issue and maybe—and to reunite her with her mother.

And, Deborah, I wish you the best.

She is studying to be a doctor.

I know you will be a very fine doctor.

You know, when I heard about these such children being kidnapped, I am sure I reacted like most people around the world, which is I thought of the time when my son was much younger and I would drop him off to school every day.

And I can't even imagine what it would be like to have learned that his entire school had been kidnapped and then maybe sold into slavery. I know that I would be screaming from the top of my lungs and insisting that this government do everything possible to get them back.

And there are some crimes against humanity that, no matter where they happen, it requires a response. And I know it is complicated, but I want to add my echo to what the chair and what so many of my colleagues said. First of all, I thank the President for sending a team, working with Israel, France, and the United Kingdom to try to bring these girls back. But as much as we can do, I want to add my voice to those who say we must bring these girls home. And, you know, this is more than just a crime against humanity.

I wanted to get into this education angle, because ''Boko Haram'' means, I think, ''Western education is a sin.'' So—because they know—they know that, when you educate children, it is a step toward freedom, democracy, and peace in the world—to have educated children, educated with a Western slant.

And so, when we ignore—when we allow children to be kidnapped because they are partaking in Western education, we are failing our own children here.

So I hope we can do more. And along those lines, I wanted to ask you—and I know this is a long-term situation.

But what are we doing to try to fight the corruption that we are finding, which seems to be endemic in so many of these governments that are having such serious problems around the world?

Ms. SEWALL. Thanks.

So, first, we don't shy away from the issue. We raise it as in the bilateral conversation because it is ultimately a limiting factor, not just in how we interact with the government, but, also, in terms of the government's ability to provide for and protect its citizens. We are vocal about our concerns.

We also work with the—with specific elements within the law enforcement sector to improve both investigatory capacity and, in many cases, judicial capacity to identify and prosecute corruption cases.

This has been a hallmark of our assistance in many different areas of the world, and it is capacity-building in a rule-bound, values-based, accountable and transparent ethos.

It is slow work. It is painstaking work. And it does ultimately require the commitment of an ever-enlarging circle of leadership within whichever country we are seeking to support anti-corruption efforts.

And many countries take different approaches to trying to address widespread and systematic corruption, and there are different degrees of successes, different approaches. So we continue to do whatever we are able.

In the case of Nigeria, it has been very specific training and capacity-building. And we will continue to press this issue because, you know, Nigeria is themost populace country in Africa.

It is, you know, an economic juggernaut, and it is extraordinarily diverse and extraordinarily important for a whole host of American security interests.

They have elections coming up in 2015. The future of democracy is very much an issue in those elections in terms of both the transparency of the elections and the risk of violence afterwards.

If Nigeria can address its corruption in a meaningful way, there is no limit on what that country can become. And it is—it is a huge opportunity there for the government to seize; so, it is very much in their interest to address it. But the conversation will be ongoing, and we will continue to press it.

Ms. FRANKEL. Thank you.

Yield back, Mr. Chair.

Chairman ROYCE. Thank you.

We go to Mr. Ted Yoho of Florida.

Mr. YOHO. Thank you, Mr. Chairman.

Doc, appreciate you sitting through this.

And I am looking at your title, Under Secretary of Civilian Security, Democracy, and Human Rights. And you have been there since February 2014. Correct?

Ms. SEWALL. Yes, sir.

Mr. YOHO. I just find it interesting when I look back over the history of Nigeria the amount of foreign aid that has been given there—it is roughly—over $400 billion, which is six times the Marshall Plan to rebuild Europe after World War II—for one country; yet, it is wrought with corruption.

And the Department Under Secretary of Civilian Security, Democracy, and Human Rights—we have been fighting that campaign for, what, 20, 30, 40 years to try to correct that problem over there?

And without putting blame on any administration, it is a problem with what we are trying to accomplish and how we go about it. We give money over and over again. Last year we gave $693 million. In 2012 we gave $647 million.

The majority of their legislators make the highest wages in any government in the world, more than the British Parliament, yet the average wage—over 70 percent of the population lives below 1.29 pounds a day, which is about—less than $4 a day.

And we are giving all this foreign aid, and then we have the situation with what we have with the Boko Haram and the situation we have with that. We are not getting to the root cause of the problem.

How do you—what do you see that we do different than what we have done in the past to change the dynamics? Because if you don't change the dynamics, nothing is going to change.

They are going to continue to kidnap people, they are going to continue to kill people, and they are going to continue to have a corrupt government. And I saw the Obama administration threaten to cut off all foreign aid to them, which I applaud.

How do we go further and change the dynamics over there? And I would like to hear what you have to say about that.

Ms. SEWALL. Sure. Well, I think, you know, again, if we parse the question a little bit in the context of what kind of aid do we provide and what do we get for it, my understanding is that the bulk of our assistance certainly now—I can't speak to 40 years ago, but certainly now—is in the realm of health assistance, significantly HIV/AIDS assistance.

Mr. YOHO. But that is going to continue. I mean, the problem is going to continue. If they don't care for their own people, we can't go in there.

We can build any school you want, but if they are going to come back there and just dismantle it, it is—what do you do to the government to change government without telling them how to live?

You know, what is that underlying cause or core value that they want to see succeed in their country for their people? And if they don't have that, we don't need to be giving them aid.

Ms. SEWALL. So the government—the government is not tearing down things. It is Boko Haram that is tearing down things.

The issue of government performance in the northeast is related to its failure to defeat Boko Haram, which has many different components, as you are alluding to.

Mr. YOHO. Boko Haram is just a fruition of government not being in check and taking care of what they need to because they are not building the infrastructure.

If they are taking all that wealth—I mean, there is $11 billion in oil money that was funneled off that went to the—to the politicians.

Back in the 1990s, there was a—the President, Sani Abacha, died in bed with two Indian prostitutes worth $4 billion.

They are not taking care of their own country and, if they don't want to take care of their own country, nothing is going to change.

And I want to know what we are going to do from a foreign policy standpoint to change the dynamics of that.

Ms. SEWALL. So one of the important changes has been the movement toward democracy. I mean, I think we can all agree that that is a significant change in the context of Nigeria's history. And so one of the more important things to do is to support a transparent and accountable democratic process.

And I spent a significant amount of time talking to the government about the upcoming 2015 elections and how it would be run and how, hopefully, they won't be disenfranchising the three states in the north by virtue of a state of emergency and how we need to be planning now—encourage them to plan now—for violence that predictably happens after the elections. So democracy is one big theme of change.

But in terms of where I think you are coming from—and then the issue of—if you have a democratic system that is vibrant, you have the ability to hold people accountable.

And so the focus that the United States has had on enhancing civil society voices to hold governments accountable and to demand greater transparency in budgets, for example, is a long-term process, but I think that is one hopeful mechanism.

Mr. YOHO. How can you do that when over 70 percent of the population is below poverty? They don't have a voice.

Ms. SEWALL. Well, in many countries, including our own, there is great income disparity. But if you have a vote, you have a vote. And so that is, I think, an important element of democracy.

I think, in terms of when I—when I look at the State Department's contributions to things that are occurring in—to capacity-building within Nigeria, I think they are in line with efforts to make the country more accountable and more responsible both as an international security actor and as a government.

So, for example, military training and education, enhancing them in their role as regional peacekeepers, antiterrorism assistance, piloting a program on woman, peace, and security, helping them in the context of their regional security responsibilities and their West African regional security responsibilities, and improving rule of law, those are the kinds of programs that the State Department facilitates that I think are necessary elements of progress.

But I agree completely with your point, and I hope I made it effectively in my opening remarks, that, ultimately, the government does need to be accountable, and corruption is an endemic problem.

Mr. YOHO. All right. I appreciate your response. I am out of time. I yield back.

Chairman ROYCE. And we are going to Steve Stockman of Texas.

Mr. STOCKMAN. I am listening to this debate, and it reminds me of the 1930s. We had a similar problem where we were trying to rationalize irrational behavior, and we didn't want to call it anything.

We have a gentleman, if you want to call him a gentleman, who is committing genocide in a country. And we can't say what his motivation is, and we know what his motivation is. You may not be able to say it, but it is hatred. And he continues to hate.

And I really resent one of my colleagues saying that our side is asking questions due to political motivation. We have the deepest compassion. We want to resolve this.

But we can't—our side—we want to—we want to support the President, but we cannot gather around a hashtag. We want to see real action, and we want to call it—we want to call it what it is.

This gentleman, or whatever you want to call him, hates. And I hear the same words coming from this administration, that they called the Speaker of the House. And the Speaker of the House they called a terrorist, and I don't think he is the same as what we are seeing in Nigeria.

And I would like to yield a minute to my colleague from Alabama to respond to, I think, unfair criticism and the balance to my friend from New Jersey.

But we have to start calling things what they are, and to equivocate on what they are and who they are is a mistake.

Ms. SEWALL. Could I just comment on that, sir?

Chairman ROYCE. Without objection, let's yield to Mr. Brooks. And then we will have the response.

Mr. BROOKS. Mr. Chairman, I take a moment to respond to the rather partisan mischaracterization and distortion of my remarks by Congressman Connolly of Virginia.

As the record shows and proves, I merely asked the witnesses to detail what the Obama administration has done or not done to encourage the United Nations in accord with the first sentence of its Charter to engage in "effective, collective measures for the prevention of threats to the peace."

Mr. Chairman, I submit that question is directed at getting the United Nations to do its job so that America does not have to once again be the only sheriff in town in something all Members of Congress of both parties can get behind without the kinds of partisan attacks and responses that were recently uttered.

Thank you for the time.

Mr. SMITH. I thank my friend for yielding.

First of all, I want to make something very clear—and this hearing has made me even more concerned than I was when I walked in the door—and that is a fundamental misread of the radical nature of Boko Haram as it relates to radical Islamic belief.

As my colleague, Mr. DeSantis, pointed out so eloquently, we have got to be able to call it for what it is. In 2012, 47 churches—Christian churches were attacked, 2 mosques; 2013, 53 churches attacked, 2 mosques.

I went to Jos. Mr. Emmanuel was there when we went to an IDP camp. We met with hundreds of Christians who were targeted for one and only one reason, because they were Christians.

And one man we brought here—and he sat where you sat—Mr. Adamu—and said they put an AK–47 to his jaw, right around his nose area, and blew his face off after he would not answer the question correctly. ''Will you convert to Islam or not?'' He said, ''No. I am ready to see my Lord. I am a Christian.'' And they blew his face away.

That is the underlying fundamental raison d'etre of Boko Haram. Yes. They hate Western education. They hate a lot of things. But at the core, as Mr. DeSantis pointed out, I think, so well, just watch what they say. It is about radical Islamic belief.

And I wish you—you know, you said you wished they would differentiate—or discriminate—they were so discriminating. Yes. They will hate other Nigerians. They will hate other Westerners. But Christians are their main targets.

Secondly, I want to strongly associate my remarks and concerns with—concerns raised by Chairman Royce that the Leahy Amendment is having the unintended consequence of precluding best practices military training of well-vetted Nigerian forces.

You said earlier—and I hope it was out of context—that it is not our problem to solve this. Well, maybe not alone, but certainly in tandem with the Nigerian Government and the families who have lost their daughters and others who may be at risk of losing their sons and daughters in the future.

One of the biggest takeaways I had on that trip was talking to our own people who said, ''Leahy is a great thing. We are all for Leahy. I voted for Leahy, would always vote for it.''

But it needs to be looked at in a calibrated fashion. There can be stood up forces in the Nigerian military who are well vetted to become a strike force and make all the difference in the world.

And maybe they are about to do that, but it should have been done for years—not months, years—and there is nothing whatsoever partisan about this. I have raised this. Members of the other side have raised first the FTO concerns.

And then we get again Johnnie Carson saying that—and I quote this because I still am amazed at this: ''The phenomenon of Boko Haram is one of discrediting the central government in power for its failure to deliver services to the people.''

That is an insult to the poor. Poor people don't join the—there is a radical Islamic perspective being promoted here and a gang-like mentality. And, of course, al-Qaeda and the like—and others like it are a part of it.

So please take back the idea of what Chairman Royce talked about because we do think, I think strongly, we have got to be able to help the military stand up capably.

I yield back.

Chairman ROYCE. Thank you.

Dr. Sewall.

Ms. SEWALL. Thank you.

And, Congressman, I appreciate your passion, and I appreciate your leadership on this issue for so very long. It is very important that Congress be participating in the formation of foreign policy.

And I want to be very clear because I don't want to be misunderstood. The question that I was asked was whether there was an official State Department position on the motivations of Boko Haram, which I simply don't have with me.

If the question is does the leadership of Boko Haram and do the actions of Boko Haram target Christianity, absolutely, unequivocally. More fundamentally, they target other things, too, and they are a threat to the government and to the region.

And so I loved the very clear-eyed characterization that was just offered, which is that Boko Haram is motivated by hatred. I don't think anybody would disagree with that. I endorse it 100 percent. And I think it simplifies the problem because we all recognize that Boko Haram is a threat that must be addressed.

I think, in terms of the Leahy Law, well-vetted units we work with—we work with now. We have been working with them for years. The problem can arise when units cannot be vetted.

But where units are vetted—and only 50 percent have not been able to be vetted—the United States is engaging in robust security cooperation.

And so I think it is just very important, as we look at the Leahy Law and as we remember that the fight in Nigeria is fundamentally about human rights and freedoms, we would wish to honor the Leahy Law's commitment to human rights in that context.

And it is only if we were to find that we could not do that, be both consistent to the Leahy Law's commitment to human rights and work in support of the human rights of Nigerians, that we would need to look at alternatives.

So I just wanted to both be very clear about my endorsement of the characterization as the motivation of Boko Haram as being hatred—and I think that is a very powerful and unifying way to think about the problem, which is a regional, if not international, problem—and agree with you that, in the context of the Leahy Law where units are well vetted, we should—and we are—work closely with them to enhance Nigeria's capacity to address this horrific threat.

Thank you.

Chairman ROYCE. Thank you, Doctor.

I am just going to clarify this point, because this testimony was as late as last week by the Defense Department testifying in the Senate.

And I will quote—because this gets back to the point at hand: ''The Leahy Law is a persistent and very troubling limitation on our ability to provide assistance, particularly training assistance that the Nigerians so badly need.''

With my opening line of questioning, I laid out the difficulty. The difficulty is finding a way for our forces to assist with the capabilities that we bring, which are unique, to help track on the ground and rescue these girls.

And so, without that waiver to come down to the bottom line, without that waiver to allow them to do that, and direction from the administration to have, you know, our Navy SEALs with this special capability that they have, you know, the ability to download information from satellite technology in the field and from drones and the ability to track in the jungle, the ability to sort of stand up that Nigerian unit and plan that operation right up to the point where Boko Haram is engaged and then allow the Nigerians to carry it out. But if we do that, then our likelihood of success is many multiples, in the viewpoint of everyone who has looked at this—many multiples of what it would be.

And since we have had the offer from the British and from the French to engage and assist, it would be very wise simply to go back, get us that waiver.

Because this is an extraordinary circumstance. I made the point before. I just want to reiterate it because I don't want us to get off the subject.

Ms. SEWALL. I didn't have a chance to respond before.

Could I respond now, Mr. Chair?

Chairman ROYCE. Yes. Absolutely.

Ms. SEWALL. Thank you so much.

So there are two different issues, and I am guessing—I am not familiar with the DoD comment, but I am guessing that the concern about Leahy as a constraint was a concern in reference to the units for whom we were unable to vet, which is some 50 percent of the Nigerian military.

I don't wish to suggest it is not a problem, but it is 50 percent. And so I just want to differentiate that from the question, which, Mr. Chairman, you are rightly putting, about the need to be cooperative in a very operational sense with the effort to return the schoolgirls.

And here we are. By virtue of an agreement that I carried with me to Abuja, we have now intelligence-sharing arrangements. We have planners——

Chairman ROYCE. Dr. Sewall, to get to the point, if you will recall my original testimony, you know what we do with the Lord's Resistance Army. We put our Special Ops in the field, on the ground, with Ugandan units and other units in order to track, in order to try to suppress Joseph Kony. Okay?

Ms. SEWALL. It is not a Leahy motivation, is what I am trying to——

Chairman ROYCE. So in this particular case, we—we have a situation where we are not doing this. What I am suggesting to you is we are not doing it.

When the issue is raised, the response is, ''Well, we would have to have a waiver to do that.'' Well, if that is the case, get a waiver, not from you——

Ms. SEWALL. I don't believe it is the case.

Chairman ROYCE. We are not doing what we need to be doing on the ground in order to track and rescue these girls. This is what this whole debate is about, not the rhetoric around it.

Ms. SEWALL. I think——

Chairman ROYCE. We are not doing it. So if you don't need a change to do it, if you don't need a waiver to do it, go back and report——

Ms. SEWALL. Yes. I will. I will take your——

Chairman ROYCE [continuing]. That, in Congress, we feel it needs to be done now.

Because the longer we wait and debate it, the farther removed these brigands get with their captives and the harder it is going to be to apprehend and rescue these girls. It should have been done immediately.

And in the future, if a situation like this comes up, I would just suggest you have the discretion. Use it. Immediately go into the field and assist in the rescue.

Now, without objection, we have a member who is not a member of this committee. But Sheila Jackson Lee wanted unanimous consent, if we could, for her to ask a question. So she might ask one question now.

Ms. JACKSON LEE. Let me thank the chairman and ranking member for their enormous courtesies.

And thank you, Dr. Sewall and Ms. Dory, for your presence here today.

I started going to Nigeria in the 1970s. I studied at their universities. And I actually stayed in the home of a family. The father was an engineer.

And I feel the consternation in this committee, but I will tell them that the enormity of people in Nigeria are not corrupt and are looking for opportunities to do what is being said in this committee, to build this country into one of the best and most productive countries for their young people, not only in Africa, but in the world.

I am very grateful for this committee that has focused on Africa with its subcommittee, but, more importantly, by its members. And I encourage our colleagues to go as you have gone and many others. I hold in my hand the list of kidnapped girls, and I do it and carry it with me all the time because these are names and people.

So I would like to pose a question around your testimony about the rescue, but more importantly as well, about the regionalism of Boko Haram from Chad to Niger to Cameroon, Togo and beyond. Ghana is not far from Nigeria.

And so the first question is—Members of Congress, women, went to the Nigerian Embassy and asked the country to establish a relief fund for the families, just announce and put in—put dollars in for the pain, the displacement—many of them may be trying to follow where the girls are, want to see whether the State Department— beyond our monies that we are giving for them to establish a relief fund.

Secondarily, in your testimony, you said that you were able to work with new battalions, special forces and Rangers. I think you were talking about in the Nigerian military, that they were established as that.

I am concerned that rescue would generate—that we would not endanger the girls. However, I do know that it is very, very concerning that there is not that concerted push using these particular battalions and special forces.

So my question is on the relief fund and how can we collaborate with the African Union on the regional aspect. Is there any grounds for the U.N. peacekeepers? I know that Ambassador Powers is not here. And is there any way that you can encourage President Jonathan that his voice now, even though it is painful—his voice continuing to speak of their concern to the world is crucial?

He made one point. And I will tell you I take a little credit for that because we were calling into Nigeria the day before the World Economic Council to indicate that he needed to say something, of which he said a little bit when he made his opening remarks. But now there is dead silence at least coming this way.

So I ask: In your engagement, can you explain to them that it is important? We know how great Nigeria's potential is and what they have done, and I want to promote it all the time.

But can we focus on this siege? Because this terrorist group is not going away unless we get our hands around it in an appropriate manner.

Ms. SEWALL. Thank you, Congresswoman.

I am not aware of any new State Department initiatives to create a victims fund, if that is the—I understand——

Ms. JACKSON LEE. No. It is for Nigeria to create a relief fund——

Ms. SEWALL. I see.

Ms. JACKSON LEE [continuing]. And for the State Department to encourage them to do something for all of those families and pronounce it publicly and nationally.

Ms. SEWALL. So I think it is fair to say that, while I did not specifically emphasize that initiative, in all of our engagements with Nigerian officials, from the President throughout the administration, we are communicating very clearly that their leadership and their vocal leadership and their expressions of empathy with the people of the northeast in the fight—who are the victims of the fight against Boko Haram is absolutely critical and that more can be done to convey both the attention and the commitment and the empathy on that point.

I think, as you point out—in terms of the regional ramifications, I believe this is a very important moment for concerned nations, if not the international community as a whole, to convince Nigeria of the need to redouble its efforts, to rethink its tactics in this fight, to flesh out its commitment to a soft approach and to identify clearly what that means in terms of the nonmilitary elements of a strategy to combat Boko Haram, to strengthen all regional platforms to both better understand the nature of the problem and to facilitate actions to address the problem concretely.

So I think this is a very important moment. And while the tragedy of the kidnapping is a heartbreak for us all, I certainly hope that we can use this as a way to do as you say, which is to improve collective efforts to address the underlying problem of Boko Haram, which is not likely to disappear in the next year.

Thank you.

Ms. JACKSON LEE. I thank the chairman very much.

And I just want to conclude by saying I heard my colleagues, and I truly believe that the religious aspect looms very large. Because this started many years back and Christians were at the direct hit of Boko Haram. It has obviously spread.

And I will finish by saying that we have tracked—and I know you have—millions of dollars that have come from the al-Qaeda structure to Boko Haram. It is really an international issue, and it really is an issue that will impact the United States maybe at some point.

And I think it is very important that we are in it for that reason and the reason for the love and need for these children to be returned to their families and the respect we have for the continent and its friendship to us.

And I yield back.

Chairman ROYCE. Well, we appreciate both of our witnesses being here this morning.

Dr. Sewall, we appreciate you finishing out the panel. Thank you very much.

The situation with these girls is critical. Members of the committee want to do all that they can to assist State and Department of Defense with any additional authority we may need in order to help secure a rescue.

What I was suggesting, the technical terminology for it, is an upgrade to an advise-and-assist role. So if that could be conveyed, I very much appreciate it.

And, also, we very much appreciate Deborah Peter being with us.

Thank you so much for your meeting with the members of our committee this morning, Deborah.

With that, we stand adjourned.

[Whereupon, at 12:24 p.m., the committee was adjourned.]

A P P E N D I X

MATERIAL SUBMITTED FOR THE RECORD

FULL COMMITTEE HEARING NOTICE
COMMITTEE ON FOREIGN AFFAIRS
U.S. HOUSE OF REPRESENTATIVES
WASHINGTON, DC 20515-6128

Edward R. Royce (R-CA), Chairman

May 21, 2014

TO: MEMBERS OF THE COMMITTEE ON FOREIGN AFFAIRS

You are respectfully requested to attend an OPEN hearing of the Committee on Foreign Affairs, to be held in Room 2172 of the Rayburn House Office Building (and available live on the Committee website at http://www.ForeignAffairs.house.gov):

DATE: Wednesday, May 21, 2014

TIME: 9:45 a.m.

SUBJECT: Boko Haram: The Growing Threat to Schoolgirls, Nigeria, and Beyond

WITNESSES: The Honorable Sarah Sewall
Under Secretary for Civilian Security, Democracy, and Human Rights
U.S. Department of State

Ms. Amanda J. Dory
Deputy Assistant Secretary of Defense for African Affairs
U.S. Department of Defense

By Direction of the Chairman

The Committee on Foreign Affairs seeks to make its facilities accessible to persons with disabilities. If you are in need of special accommodations, please call 202/225-5021 at least four business days in advance of the event, whenever practicable. Questions with regard to special accommodations in general (including availability of Committee materials in alternative formats and assistive listening devices) may be directed to the Committee.

COMMITTEE ON FOREIGN AFFAIRS
MINUTES OF FULL COMMITTEE HEARING

Day _Wednesday_ Date _05/21/14_ Room _2172_

Starting Time _9:53 a.m._ Ending Time _12:24 p.m._

Recesses _0_ (___to___) (___to___) (___to___) (___to___) (___to___) (___to___)

Presiding Member(s)

Edward R. Royce, Chairman

Check all of the following that apply:

Open Session ☑   Electronically Recorded (taped) ☑
Executive (closed) Session ☐   Stenographic Record ☑
Televised ☑

TITLE OF HEARING:

Boko Haram: The Growing Threat to Schoolgirls, Nigeria, and Beyond

---

COMMITTEE MEMBERS PRESENT:

See Attendance Sheet.

NON-COMMITTEE MEMBERS PRESENT:

Rep. Sheila Jackson Lee

HEARING WITNESSES: Same as meeting notice attached? Yes ☑ No ☐
(If "no", please list below and include title, agency, department, or organization.)

STATEMENTS FOR THE RECORD: _(List any statements submitted for the record.)_

Connolly

TIME SCHEDULED TO RECONVENE _____
or
TIME ADJOURNED _12:24 p.m._

Edward Burrier, Deputy Staff Director

HOUSE COMMITTEE ON FOREIGN AFFAIRS
FULL COMMITTEE HEARING

PRESENT	MEMBER	PRESENT	MEMBER
X	Edward R. Royce, CA	X	Eliot L. Engel, NY
X	Christopher H. Smith, NJ		Eni F.H. Faleomavaega, AS
	Ileana Ros-Lehtinen, FL	X	Brad Sherman, CA
X	Dana Rohrabacher, CA	X	Gregory W. Meeks, NY
	Steve Chabot, OH	X	Albio Sires, NJ
	Joe Wilson, SC	X	Gerald E. Connolly, VA
X	Michael T. McCaul, TX	X	Theodore E. Deutch, FL
X	Ted Poe, TX		Brian Higgins, NY
X	Matt Salmon, AZ		Karen Bass, CA
	Tom Marino, PA		William Keating, MA
X	Jeff Duncan, SC	X	David Cicilline, RI
X	Adam Kinzinger, IL		Alan Grayson, FL
X	Mo Brooks, AL	X	Juan Vargas, CA
X	Tom Cotton, AR	X	Bradley S. Schneider, IL
X	Paul Cook, CA	X	Joseph P. Kennedy III, MA
X	George Holding, NC	X	Ami Bera, CA
X	Randy K. Weber, Sr., TX	X	Alan S. Lowenthal, CA
X	Scott Perry, PA		Grace Meng, NY
X	Steve Stockman, TX	X	Lois Frankel, FL
X	Ron DeSantis, FL	X	Tulsi Gabbard, HI
X	Doug Collins, GA		Joaquin Castro, TX
X	Mark Meadows, NC		
X	Ted S. Yoho, FL		
	Luke Messer, IN		

MATERIAL SUBMITTED FOR THE RECORD BY THE HONORABLE EDWARD R. ROYCE, A REPRESENTATIVE IN CONGRESS FROM THE STATE OF CALIFORNIA, AND CHAIRMAN, COMMITTEE ON FOREIGN AFFAIRS

Congressional Testimony of Deborah Peters

ON BOKO HARAM: THE GROWING THREAT TO SCHOOLGIRLS, NIGERIA, AND BEYOND

Before the

Committee on Foreign Affairs

U.S. House of Representatives

May 21, 2014

MY STORY

My name is Deborah Peter and I am the sole survivor of a Boko Haram attack on my household.

On December 22, 2011 at 7 pm, my brother and I were at home when we started hearing some guns shooting. My brother called my dad and told him not to come home because some people were shooting guns. But my dad said he should not worry because it was not the first time he had come home when people were fighting. When my dad came home, he said that he was going to take a shower because he was hot.

At 7:30 pm, three men knocked on the door. My brother answered the door because he recognized one of the men as a Muslim in our community. The men asked where my dad was and I told them that he was in the shower. The men waited. After three minutes, they went into the bathroom and dragged my dad into the main room. They said that my dad was wasting their time and that they did not have time to wait on him. The men told my dad that he should deny his Christian faith. My dad told them that he would not deny his faith. They said that if he did not deny his faith they were going to kill him. My dad refused, saying that Jesus said whoever acknowledges Him in front of man, He will acknowledge in front of God; and whoever denies Him in front of man, He will deny in front of God in heaven. My dad said that he would rather die than go to hell fire. After he told the men that, the men shot him three times in his chest.

My brother was in shock. He started demanding, "What did my dad do to you? Why did you shoot him?" The men told him to be quiet or else they were going to shoot him too. Then, the men discussed whether they should kill my brother. One of the Boko Harams said they should kill Caleb, my brother. The second man said that he was just a boy and that he was too young to kill. But the third man said that they should make an exception in this case because Caleb will only grow up to be a Christian pastor. Caleb asked me to plead with them for his life but they told me to shut up or they would kill me too. The leader agreed that they should kill him and shot my brother two times. My dad had still been breathing but when he saw them shoot Caleb, he died.

My brother fell down but was still alive and gasping. The men shot him in his mouth. Then, my brother stopped moving and died. I was in shock. I did not know what was happening. The men put me in the middle of my dad and brother's corpses, told me to be quiet or be killed, and left me there. I stayed there until the next day when the army came. They removed my dad and brother's bodies to the mortuary and took me to the hospital.

I was traumatized. A nearby pastor paid for me to get out of town when he discovered that Boko Haram said they made a mistake by not also killing me. Boko Haram decided later that they should have killed me because I am the daughter of an apostate Muslim mother who converted to Christianity. So the pastor paid for me to get out of that region. I fled and Jubilee Campaign helped me come to a 9/11 child survivors of terrorism camp in America. On May 15, 2013, that pastor, Rev Faye Pama, was killed by Boko Haram in front of his kids.

Similar to that pastor, my family was targeted by Boko Haram because we are Christians. My dad was a pastor. We had to move from place to place because Boko Haram always attacked my father and told him that they would kill him. In November, they burned his church and threatened him. My dad refused to deny his faith and rebuilt his church. That is why they killed him—because he is a Christian.

I decided to tell the world my story when the Chibok girls were taken because everyone needs to know how horrible Boko Haram is. They kill innocent people who never hurt them. I want the world to understand what happened to me. I hope that the kidnapped Chibok girls will take courage from my story, and know more of what God says, and know what it means to stand strong in the face of bad people. I hope that they will be free and be able to go to school and worship freely. I hope that like me, some of them can come and continue their education in America.

My mum graduated from the school from which they were kidnapped. Chibok is a small town where everyone is related to everyone else and although it is majority Christian, everyone lived in peace until book Haram came. I know at least one of the kidnapped school girls named Hauwa. I pray for them and ask everyone to pray for them too.

I am thankful to Tuesday's Children, the 911 Foundation for inviting me to a summer camp for child survivors of terrorism, I am thankful to Jubilee Campaign for bringing me to America and I am thankful to Mt Mission School for giving me a chance to continue my education and being a home to me in America.

Thank you.

Statement for the Record
Submitted by the Honorable Gerald Connolly

On May 9, 2014, this committee passed H. Res. 573 introduced by my colleague Ms. Wilson of Florida. I was proud to cosponsor the resolution which condemned the abduction of schoolgirls in Nigeria by the terrorist group Boko Haram, supported United States assistance for Nigeria's search for the girls and commended United States operations that hold this abhorrent group accountable for the violence it has perpetrated on the Nigerian people.

In H. Res. 573, this committee proclaimed a value that is by no means groundbreaking, but when violated can be earth shattering.

> *Resolved, That the House of Representatives -*
> *(6) recognizes that every individual, regardless of gender, should have the opportunity to pursue an education without fear of discrimination.*

On Sunday, this proud father watched his only daughter walk the Lawn at the University of Virginia and receive her Masters in Public Policy. It has always been my hope that educational opportunities afforded to her in life will be determined by her character and work ethic, and never denied to her by prejudice. Working towards that end is good parenting, and it is good public policy.

Equal access to education in foreign countries is fundamental to our foreign policy goals to advance civil society and promote democratic participation. Unfortunately, disparities in education between the genders exist around the world with women accounting for almost two-thirds of the world's 792 million illiterate adults, according to the UN. In some cases such disparities are due to an active and insidious effort to suppress female literacy. Boko Haram is one such organization that uses violence to deny women an education.

This is particularly troubling in light of the fact that female literacy rates in sub-Saharan Africa are already among the lowest in the world and there persists a staggering literacy gap between the genders in some sub-Saharan countries. In Nigeria, female and male literacy rates stand at 50.4 percent and 72.1 percent, respectively. For bordering country Niger, those figures are 15.1 percent and 42.9 percent and for Benin they are 33.2 percent and 55.2 percent. Reaching even these levels was a hard-fought battle waged over the past two decades to raise literacy rates by 9 percent in sub-Saharan Africa.

An organization like Boko Haram that undermines the basic tenets of fair education is in direct conflict with our mission abroad. I hope our witnesses from the U.S. Department of State and U.S. Department of Defense can discuss our efforts to counter this threat. I would be particularly interested in hearing about developments from the weekend regarding a multilateral initiative to engage Boko Haram in Nigeria and neighboring countries. We must return these girls to their families and set them back on the path to advancement and full participation in society. I thank you for your insight and look forward to your testimony.